Things I Know Now
That I Wish I'd Known Then

THINGS I KNOW NOW THAT I WISH I'D KNOWN THEN

---

150 Tips for Living Smarter

---

by

GEORGE NEWMAN

Robert D. Reed Publishers
P.O. Box 1992
Bandon, OR 97411
Phone: 541-347-9882 • Fax: -9883
E-mail: 4bobreed@msn.com
web site: www.rdrpublishers.com

Typesetting: Barbara Kruger, Nancy Solomon
Cover Design: Grant Prescott
Illustrations: Hugh Armstrong

ISBN 1-931741-66-2

Library of Congress Control Number 2005934543

Manufactured, typeset and printed in the United States of America

For Jacque Fresco

Contents

Life Skills

Your Health

Business

Time Savers

Author's Note

If you're reading this book, there's a good chance that you and I have a lot in common. We work at finding opportunities others miss. We subscribe to financial publications, health newsletters and read newspapers. And we buy books like this one.

Why do we do these things? So we can live life smarter and avoid the high-priced penalties that the uninformed must pay. It's always been a mystery to me why so many people will depart on a vacation equipped with maps and tour books, but allocate no thought whatever toward a plan for getting through life.

The philosopher George Santayana wrote, "Those who do not learn from the lessons of history are condemned to repeat its failures."

This book is filled with *my* "history." I invite you to go ahead—profit from my mistakes. Learn from my lessons without having to experience the pitfalls yourself. Take advantage of some insider knowledge that can provide you with an edge.

Not every idea or technique here is original. It's likely you've already discovered a few of these on your own. But, you'll find many great tips that are new to you and will help you save time, money and frustration.

I would like to acknowledge the ongoing encouragement, support and counsel of my wife, Sondra; the advice of my son, Rick, and my friend, Bob Reed; and the editing skills and experience of my friends, Dale Rodebaugh and Marian Sanders.

Tucson, Arizona
March, 2006

Dollars and Sense

1

Never Pay Bank Fees

I'm astounded at the number of people who maintain personal checking accounts at the largest banking chains which, with few exceptions, charge the highest fees and offer the fewest free services. Some of these mega-banks have become so profit-conscious that they charge customers to simply enter their lobbies, talk to a live teller or use their automated telephone menu (usually after a limited number of free phone calls). Also, you can usually count on waiting in line longer and being treated impersonally.

I never consider doing business with a large banking chain, and in the last forty years I have never paid a banking fee. I first look in the Yellow Pages for banks or savings and loan associations and start phoning. I tell whoever answers the phone that I'm looking for the lowest possible monthly fee—preferably no fee at all—with the lowest required balance. Invariably, I'll get the best deal from a small, locally-owned independent bank, savings and loan or credit union.

Also, check the bank and S&L ads in your newspaper's financial section and watch for a special offer. Periodically, a bank, an S&L, or sometimes a credit union will offer free checking or charter checking. The latter means that if you open an account as a charter member (when a new bank or reorganized bank first opens its doors) you will be guaranteed a free checking account until you close the account. I opened such a checking account with a bank in California 34 years ago and although I no longer live in that state, I continue to maintain the account—free of monthly fees, of course. If you're paying, let's say, $10.00 a month for personal checking and you figure it costs you $120.00 a year, multiply that number by 34 years. It's a savings of $4,080.00. Can you think of some things that you could do with that money other than pay checking charges?

2

Time Is Money

How much time do you waste running an errand for a single purchase? Whenever possible, my wife and I don't get into our cars until we have a list of several errands. One of us will take all errands that are concentrated in a specific area of our community, while the other takes those which are in the opposite direction. If grocery shopping is included, the market is always the last stop on the list because of transporting perishables.

Also, if possible, try to do your grocery shopping once a week or twice at most. The only valid reason for grocery shopping every day is to get out of the house for the enjoyment of human contact. My wife and I save many valuable hours by consolidating our errands. And since time is money, we can use our time saved more productively.

3

How to Save $250,000

Many people I know buy a new car every three or four years. I'm aware that there are many pleasures, comforts and conveniences that go along with a new car. But at what cost?

Some friends, who, like my wife and I, don't trade in their cars often, came up with some interesting figures. They found data showing that if you buy a new car every ten years, instead of every three years, you'll save $250,000 to $300,000 in your lifetime. And if you're a young person reading this, the figure might reach $500,000. Consider what that money invested in other than new cars can do for you.

P.S. If you're concerned about needing a car to take that once-or-twice-a-year road trip, see Chapter 30, "Own an Old Car, Rent a New Car."

4

Shop on the Day after Christmas

It's no secret to most people that there are huge shopping bargains available the day after Christmas. What's not commonly known is that by taking full advantage of the sales you can save a bundle.

This means not only buying your Christmas cards and decorations for next year, but also buying most, if not all, of next year's Christmas gifts at discounts of 50 percent or more.

It's difficult for many of us to envision shopping a year ahead, but when you consider that there's often some very attractive merchandise offered at deep discounts, it pays.

On December 26, you'll find these bargains throughout most shopping malls. Buy what you'll need next Christmas, take it home and find a convenient storage location where the items will be protected. Next November, check your storage and begin getting ready for the holidays.

5

Offer Cash

Before buying a big-ticket item such as an appliance, carpeting, car or furniture, ask if there is a discount for paying cash. It could be a good deal for you *and* the merchant who otherwise must pay his credit card company a fee of three or four percent of the purchase price.

Don't be shy, but be polite. I once hesitated to ask about a cash discount. A friend who accompanied me advised, "George, ask the question. The man can say 'yes' or he can say 'no.'"

I asked and received a two percent discount.

6

I Want It Now!

Instant gratification is possible, but it costs. If you use a credit card and fail to pay your monthly statement in full, you face interest payments of up to 30 percent annually.

In addition to a debt that seems to go on forever, credit-card users often end up paying twice as much as those who paid cash.

Buying on credit has become a way of life, but debts are a mortgage on your future. They can force you to stay in a job that you detest or cause stress from worrying about unpaid bills.

Debts also give others power over you. You can't tell your boss how you really feel about something or he might fire you. Or perhaps, your in-laws have loaned you money?

I use a credit card for convenience. I pay the bill in full at the end of the month and I don't buy anything that I can't afford. Real estate is the only exception, and I pay down my mortgages as quickly as possible.

I have never paid monthly fees or a service charge. Many people could probably quit smoking or shed 40 pounds easier than they could switch to debt-free living. But, there are those, like myself, who wouldn't live any other way.

7

No Honest Job Is Beneath You

Sometimes the least glamorous types of work—especially the dirty-hands variety—are the best paying and most secure. Many people earn an advanced college degree and at age 25 or 30 enter the job market with high expectations. With some exceptions, they find that their MBA or advanced degrees in fine arts are a dime a dozen. Often what's available are service jobs in banks or at large discount retailers. Many hire only part-time employees to avoid paying health care and other benefits—usually at slightly above minimum wage.

Also, in the current corporate world, employees often are dumped onto the rubbish heap after years of loyal service as a result of downsizing, outsourcing or export of their jobs abroad. They find themselves virtually unemployable—except at low-paying positions—while not yet old enough to retire.

In contrast, consider the plumber. His time is billed at $65 an hour, plus a minimum-service charge, just to repair a kitchen faucet. During the many years I managed rental property, I noticed that the skilled tradesmen were always as busy as they wanted to be—whether in recession or boom. There's no correlation between leaky roofs or plugged toilets and the economy.

I once talked with a man in Sacramento, California, who operated his own sewer and drain cleaning service. He had five trucks on the road and drove a sixth himself. He explained that he held an MBA and had once been offered a position in the corporate world. "I take some kidding about the smell," he confided. "But, I laugh all the way to the bank." Also, he doesn't lie awake nights worrying that his job might be exported to a country where the work can be done cheaper.

I have often joked with a friend in the publishing field that had we entered the business of dipping wooden utility poles into creosote, we undoubtedly would have enjoyed greater financial success and stability.

Most people simply don't want to get their hands dirty, so look for the jobs that few others consider and that are minimally affected by economic swings or foreign trade policy.

8

Grocery Coupons

I have a little extra jingle in my pocket because I clip grocery coupons, which saves me about $500 a year. Without them, I would have to earn an additional $700 to have $500—after taxes—to buy those same groceries.

Most grocery chains in our area offer "double coupons" and sometimes "triple coupons." In addition, many of the chains issue their own coupon books full of specials. The grocery chains' coupons are known as "store coupons" while the coupons printed in the Sunday newspaper are "manufacturers' coupons." What a lot of people don't know is that many grocery chains will allow a customer to use a store coupon *and* a manufacturer's coupon toward the purchase of a single item.

Take for example a jar of XYZ brand applesauce that regularly retails for $2.29. A store coupon allows you to buy the applesauce on special for $1.49 while a manufacturer's coupon offers a 50-cent discount on the same product. If the store has a double-coupon policy, the checker will double the value of the manufacturer's coupon, giving you a $1.00 additional savings. Deduct $1.00 from the store's special price of $1.49 and you end up paying 49 cents for the applesauce.

Manufacturer's coupons are also available for purchase in quantity at a fraction of their face value from several commercial services. Many of these can be found on the Internet. Also, coupons are often sold by nonprofit organizations.

9

Floating Gifts

Floating gifts—ones that you can't use and intend to recycle—are nothing new, but here's a suggestion that can save you embarrassment.

Always tag a floating gift, using a Post-It note or some other tag secured by a string, or tape so that it can't fall off and leave you wondering who gave it to you. On the tag, write the name of the giver and the date received.

When you decide to pass the gift along to another person, be sure that the recipient is someone who is not acquainted with the original giver. The reason should be obvious.

10

A Tale of Two Households

Some years ago, a neighbor—we'll call him Kurt—whose income was double my own, asked me how I could afford to live as well as he did on half the income. I replied that I did it by spending money wisely. Some examples:

- Kurt kept his account at a big name bank and paid about $12 every month in fees. I maintain a checking account at a small bank where there is no minimum fee or service charge.
- Kurt charged vacation trips to his credit card and paid 18.9 percent interest on the balance, sometimes taking up to two years to pay off his trip. I only buy what I can pay for within 30 days. Each month, I pay my credit card bill in full. I pay no annual fee for my credit card. The only interest charges I've ever paid were on home mortgages.
- Kurt, on impulse, bought a set of luggage at regular price (about $300 for three pieces), charged the amount to his credit card and then paid it off at 18.9 percent interest. His thrifty neighbor—me—waited until the luggage went on sale and bought an identical set for about $150. In the end, Kurt paid almost $450 for the luggage, including interest charges.
- When Kurt goes on a trip, he returns home to find his mailbox filled with overdue bills. Most of these bills include a late charge which Kurt must pay. When I go on vacation, I estimate the amount of my upcoming bills, always adding a little extra, and pay before I leave. This requires planning at least 30 days

in advance. If I'm paying an electric power bill or phone bill, I choose to err on the side of paying too much. The overpayment is credited to my account. But, if I forget, and the bill is overdue when I return home, I'll pay a hefty late fee.

And where is Kurt today? The last time I saw him he had maxed out his credit cards, filed for bankruptcy and moved in with his wife's parents.

11

Ask for That Discount!

Don't be shy about asking for discounts. They are available in the most unexpected places. If you are 55 or older, always ask for a senior citizen discount. Often, even if the required age is 60 or 65, a discount will be extended to almost anyone with graying hair who asks for it. Remember, the worst that can happen is that someone will say "no." Discounts are often available to students (including mature adults if they are enrolled students) and active and retired military personnel.

When you buy from an owner-operator, you can often negotiate for a discount if you are purchasing more than one item. For example, "If I take the washer, the dryer, oven, refrigerator and freezer, can you give me a package price?" In my experience, the answer is always "yes." At most chain stores, the answer is almost a certain "no." Chain store employees, including managers, seldom have discretion to allow such discounts.

12

Stock Up

Just as important as organizing your errands to save time is stocking up on items you regularly use. That saves you both time and money. The next time you're in the store, buy three or four or a dozen of your favorite products—even if they're not on sale. The time you save by not making that extra trip is far more valuable than the pennies you might have saved on the purchase. You'll also avoid what I call the "incompetency crisis in America." When I go shopping and ask a question of a store employee (that's assuming I can find one), a common reply is, "If you don't see it, we don't have it." You can cut down on the number of such replies by loading up on what you need and use most often.

It's best to stock up on items that have a long shelf life and can be stored at room temperature. Also create a backup supply of clothing and shoes that you need. During the hot summers in Arizona, I always wear a blue chambray work shirt and tropic-weight khaki pants. Of course, they're 100 percent cotton. Also, I have some very comfortable shoes to go along with this outfit. Unfortunately, I've discovered—the hard way—that manufacturers and retail stores are constantly introducing new merchandise and phasing out the old. When I go back to the same store a year later, I often find that the item I want has been discontinued. Having learned my lesson, if I find an item of clothing or pair of shoes that I really like, I buy several at that moment, knowing that a year later I might not be able to buy more. And, if I find that the item(s) happen to be on sale, it's a double savings.

My all-time coup—in terms of saving *both* time and money—occurred some years ago as a result of a tip whispered to me by a barber. He had completed my haircut, and I had asked to buy some shampoo to use at home. The barber was an employee, not the owner of the shop, so he whispered in my ear that I could buy a gallon of shampoo concentrate at the barber and beauty supply store across the street and save a bundle. He was right. I purchased the gallon of concentrate. It was a quality name brand and every month I mixed a small amount with water into a plastic squeeze bottle which I kept in the shower. I shampooed every day, and at the end of a year the gallon of concentrate was *still* almost full. At the end of sixteen years, I poured the last measure of concentrate into the squeeze bottle. My cost for the gallon of concentrate: $16.00 plus tax. That breaks down to $1.00 per year for daily shampoo expense over the sixteen-year period. I love to tell this story!

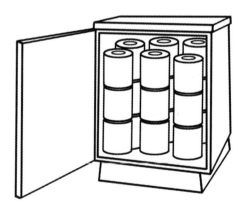

13

Pay Off Your Mortgage

Most financial experts say that it's not wise to pay off a home mortgage early. Some even suggest that upon paying off a mortgage, the homeowner should immediately refinance to enjoy the benefit of deducting mortgage interest. While such a tactic may benefit people in high income brackets or those in unusual tax circumstances, one size doesn't fit all.

I contend that a majority of homeowners would find their financial position improved by *paying off* their mortgages—and the sooner, the better. Here's why: If your mortgage is paid off and you're laid off from work or forced into early retirement, you won't lose sleep worrying about that big monthly payment. Further, if you no longer have a mortgage, you gain added independence in your day-to-day financial decisions as well as those affecting your job.

Let's say you are retired or have been forced to live on reduced income due to job downsizing or other economic factors. And let's say that your monthly mortgage payment is $1,400. Question: How much would you need to earn in gross income to make that $1,400 payment? Answer: Probably around $2,000, taking into account federal, state and local taxes, Social Security and Medicare deductions. But if your house is already paid off, you don't have to worry about a $2,000-a-month ax over your head. It's true that you no longer have a mortgage deduction, but calculate how much you're saving by not having to earn the $2,000 required to make such a mortgage payment.

Admittedly, there are exceptions. One is the person with a reliable stream of income who, at the same time, is in a position to invest money borrowed on a mortgage refinance and receive a higher rate of investment return than he is paying on the mortgage loan. And, of course, there are others.

14

The 'Cheap Furniture Law'

I have my Uncle Max to thank for alerting me to the fact that quality items pay for themselves, often many times over. That wisdom was acquired when I was a bachelor trying to furnish my first house. I was having a difficult time making a hefty mortgage payment, and the house was bare for a long time except for the basics—a bed, nightstand and a kitchen dinette set.

One Saturday morning, just prior to getting into the car to go shopping for furniture, I was counseled via long-distance by Uncle Max, the family patriarch. He said to me: "My boy, buy only the best quality furniture. You cannot *afford* cheap furniture."

It wasn't until years later that the full meaning of his advice made an impact. Uncle Max's "Cheap Furniture Law," of course, applies to almost all purchases we make. At the time, however, after viewing flimsy excuses for what was termed "furniture" at several discount stores, I decided to make the rounds of garage sales. Finally, I came across a good quality sofa and a dining room set that had been gently used. I bought them, paying only a fraction of the price of new pieces. These additions lasted for years and they looked great.

Now, whenever my wife and I buy furniture, appliances, hot water heaters or cars, we always rank quality and durability as our highest priority. Do you realize what you spend on repair or replacement of cheap equipment? For example, the labor cost for one service call is usually much more than the difference between what you would pay for a hot water heater with a five-year warranty and a top-of-the-line model that offers a 15-year warranty. Thanks, Uncle Max.

15

When to Say 'Charge It'

When you use a credit card to pay for major purchases, you'll have extra protection in case something goes wrong. Even if you pay your bill in full every month to avoid interest or service charges, you'll still benefit from paying by credit card.

For example, let's say you buy a new computer and it's a lemon. There's a warranty, but you can't seem to get satisfaction from the company that sold it to you. If you paid by check or cash, aside from complaining to company management, your only recourse is through the courts. And as we all know, filing a lawsuit can be an expensive proposition, even if you win in court.

But, if you charge the purchase to your credit card, you have additional leverage. Often, simply informing the seller that you intend to file a complaint for recovery with your credit card company is enough to get attention, and sometimes it will prompt an offer to make good on the faulty merchandise. If the seller doesn't respond favorably, you can file your complaint with your credit card issuer.

Most banks and credit card companies have established procedures for resolving such disputes. If, after investigating, your credit card issuer determines that your claim is justified, it can often recover the amount you paid directly from the merchant's bank—without need of legal action. The amount can then be credited to your credit card account. This doesn't mean that in each and every case your credit card issuer will decide that you are entirely right or that you'll receive a full refund. But, using a credit card can assure you access to recourses you wouldn't have otherwise.

16

Pay 'Real People' First

If you're like most of us, there are times when you are unable to pay all of your bills promptly. Sometimes they stack up. You wait to pay some bills until next payday or when an income tax refund check arrives. So, how do you decide which bills to pay when there isn't enough money to pay all of them?

My policy is to pay individuals first—real people. They appreciate your payments more than the computer that processes your check at a large corporation. Often, for "real people"—your plumber, dentist or dry cleaner—your payment can actually make a difference in their lives. That's not to say that you should shrug off payments such as a home mortgage, car payment or insurance premium. Such could result in serious consequences, including foreclosure or a negative credit record.

The factors I consider in deciding who to pay first are: (1) payment due date; (2) consequences of paying late; (3) possibility of requesting and receiving an extension; (4) to whom or to what company is the payment going and how important is it that I keep the good will of this individual or company? I always try to mail a check to the handyman who repairs my garage door or clothes washer on the day after his bill is received. If my monthly credit card bill is due on the last day of the month, I will make sure that it's paid by that date. However, I won't pay the credit card charge early unless I don't need the money for anything else. A credit rating is based on whether you pay on time or pay late. There's no reward for paying credit card statements early.

17

Free Directory Assistance

Why pay for a phone number? Phone companies now charge $1.50 or more to look up a single number for you. Years ago, this information was free. But, you can do something about it. All you need is a computer and you can look them up yourself for free.

Several websites offer free telephone directory information. They include InfoUSA.com, Bigfoot.com, Smartpages.com and Switchboard.com. There are others, and new websites come online frequently.

On some of these websites you'll need to register first or navigate your way through to the white pages or yellow pages, depending on your needs. It may take a bit of searching to find a free website where you're comfortable. However, once you've found the one that's right for you, add it to your list of "favorites." You'll find yourself saving money immediately. My wife and I look up phone numbers at least twice a week. That represents a minimum savings of $300 per year. Not exactly small change.

There are also free websites for looking up phone numbers in Canada and other foreign countries.

If you don't own a computer, ask a relative or friend who has a computer to look up a phone number for you. Or use the computer at the nearest public library.

18

A Penny Saved

Americans today are among the worst savers in the world. One study shows that our average savings rate is on the negative side of the chart. In other words, as a nation, we spend more than we earn.

I can't remember what motivated me, but as a young man, I decided that it was better to live *below* my means. The motivation might have stemmed from an experience I had while working as a temporary employee on a county government survey crew.

One day at lunch, I heard an older man, who was part of our team, tell an acquaintance why he was working at such a menial job. He explained that two years earlier, as a real estate agent, he'd earned $60,000 and began to live like someone making $60,000. The next year, he said, due to a downturn in the real estate market, he earned only $6,000 and lost everything—house, vacation condo and the Mercedes. A change in fortune can happen to anyone, especially in an unstable economy.

Another time, I worked with a man who seemed untroubled about having bills far in excess of his ability to pay. I once asked him whether being in debt didn't worry him. He laughed. "I don't worry. I let my creditors worry," he said.

The reverse side of this coin—having savings in reserve for a rainy day—enables you to say "no" to a boss or "no" to a customer on whose business you depend. Needless to say, most of us won't have those resources available if we, at the same time, try to maintain a lifestyle more appropriate for the rich and famous.

19

Bigger Isn't Always Better

I learned when I was a youngster that bigger isn't always better. During summers, I bought peaches, plums, grapes and cherries when I wanted something sweet (I didn't like candy). I quickly discovered that the higher-priced, larger pieces of fruit didn't taste any better than the smaller pieces. In fact, they were often *not* as sweet or juicy.

I've seen grocery stores sell large grapefruit for $1.29 per pound and slightly smaller ones for 39 cents a pound. This tells me that buyers want big pieces of fruit, so stores must increase the price on the larger pieces and cut the price on the smaller ones to balance supply and demand.

Often the best buy on apples or oranges are those that come in a plastic bag weighing three pounds. The price per pound for these is substantially less than that charged for the larger pieces which you select individually. The same rule applies to many other foods and products.

P.S. Because I enjoy eating fruit that's sweet and has character, I always search the produce bins for all the ripe fruit that I can find.

20

Too Good to Be True

Adages endure because they are timeless kernels of wisdom. Take, for example, "If it seems too good to be true, it usually is too good to be true."

In past years, I can't recall more than a couple offers that have come in the mail, via telephone solicitation, or Internet spam that have merited consideration. When any offer seems too good to be true, your suspicion index should rise immediately to its highest level. If after investigating thoroughly, you are still prone to move ahead, contact your lawyer first and also seek the opinions of a few of your wise friends or relatives.

21

Becky Is My 'Banker'

As a corollary to finding the best bank, it's also wise to find a "personal banker." Banks often use this term to promote their services, but people I know report that it's so much fluff. It reads well in their ads, but in reality there's not much to it. You might receive someone's personal business card, but with employee turnover what it is, the person may be history in a month or two.

My own version of a personal banker is simply a bank employee, a teller, an assistant manager, or anyone who gives you a warm smile and a hello. In my case, that's Becky—a friendly and efficient teller at our bank. I make an effort to take my deposits to her each time I visit the bank. I don't have to fish out identification every time I need to cash a check or receive cash back from a deposit. If I have a problem or question, I contact Becky in person or by phone. She knows me now and is always very helpful.

If your contact in the bank does a small favor for you, be sure to follow with a nice thank-you note. Should you find yourself receiving extra-special service from that employee, you might wish to include him or her on your list for Christmas candy or fruitcakes. Don't deliver or mail the gift to the bank. Instead, tell the employee that you would like to add his or her name to your Christmas list and could you send your mail to them at their home address?

22

'I Always Overpay!'

Being a tightwad with service personnel is a fast way to lose the good will of the people you count on for vital assistance. I learned this while visiting my Aunt Lizzie, an old-age pensioner, who required help to maintain her household in a London suburb.

A cleaning woman who had worked for her more than 20 years rearranged her schedule and found time to increase her visits from once to three times a week when the need arose. Additionally, the cleaning woman's husband, a retired transport worker, stopped by a couple times a week to help my aunt do her grocery shopping and drive her to appointments.

One afternoon as the cleaning woman was departing, my aunt handed her a check for her week's work. When the woman protested that it was more than she usually received, my aunt simply noted that she had recently worked some extra time. After the woman departed, my aunt said to me matter-of-factly, "I always overpay. I appreciate her loyalty and service and this is how I let her know it."

In contrast, another elderly woman I knew, who was affluent, constantly haggled over small amounts with her day help. She went through domestics at the rate of about one per month. Pennywise and pound-foolish?

23

Timing Is Everything

I don't want to overwork this, but here again is an approach to saving money by taking advantage of timing. Suppose you want your house painted or re-roofed. The quote you get may often depend on *when* you approach the contractor. If the contractor is busy, he may quote you a higher price than he would if business were slow.

On several occasions, contractors have acknowledged to me that they underbid their competitors by several hundred dollars because they had a couple of good workers who weren't doing anything and they wanted to keep them busy.

They'd profit little or nothing on such a job, the aim being instead to provide steady employment for their workers. Then, when business returns to normal, the boss won't have to go out recruiting new employees.

Timing is important and can make a difference in how much you pay.

Traveling Smart

24

Bargain Hotel Rates

Most people don't know this, but there can be as many as four or five different rates for every room in a hotel or resort—much like for seats on an airplane. When you plan to travel, compile a list of possible lodgings, getting a local as well as a toll-free telephone number for each one. For lowest rates, try to arrange your trip so that you arrive on a Friday, and ask about weekend rates.

Try the toll-free number first. Usually, it will be a central reservations service for the entire chain. Tell the reservationist that you are "shopping" and that you need a quote for the very lowest price possible. Ask about special weekend rates and possible additional discounts, such as for AAA or AARP membership.

Next, place a call directly to the hotel. Yes, it will cost you for the long-distance, but it's worth it. Repeat the same questions, again making sure that you emphasize that you are shopping for the lowest-priced room. Odds are that you'll hear a different price than you were quoted by the central reservations agent.

If you're online, check the chain's website and search for their lowest rate. Also, try some of the super-bargain websites that allow you to submit an offer for a rock-bottom room rate, though you must be careful and familiarize yourself with the website's rules. After you've compared the different quoted rates, you can make a better decision.

25

Saving at Resorts

Shopping for reduced rates at resorts is different than hunting for hotel bargains in the city. Most people want to visit resorts on the weekends. So, naturally, the best rates are during the slow period—the middle of the week.

In the cities, it's the opposite. Business travelers want to be at home on the weekends, so the city hotels are often sparsely occupied then.

Many resorts are not affiliated with chains, so often there's no need to look for a central reservations phone number. Instead, telephone the resort directly. Some offer a toll-free number. Ask the same questions you used with the hotels, again being sure to emphasize that you are shopping for the lowest rate possible for a mid-week stay. Also, ask if there are any special promotion packages available.

26

Don't Fly at Sky-High Fares

Relying solely on an airline's central reservations desk for ticket fares is not wise. Once you decide where you're going, phone an airline and say that you want the lowest fare available. Then, contact a travel agent about the same itinerary. You are certain to get a different quote. After that, if you have online access, click on one or more of the websites which offer fare comparisons and travel discounts. Next, call a competing airline and again say you are shopping for the lowest fare. Finally, phone the airline that you started with, but this time share with the agent what you have meanwhile discovered and emphasize that you're shopping for the best deal. It's not uncommon to end up with an even lower fare.

But, don't make a decision yet. Wait a day or two and repeat the same steps because many air carriers change rates as often as every twenty-four hours for certain flights and certain seats. At this point, you will have a good overview of fares. It may require a few more phone calls, but you could end up saving a substantial amount. There are often dozens of different air fares between two points and the airlines don't always make that information easily accessible. For that reason alone, it pays to inquire and then inquire further.

In renting a car, there's no advantage to phoning a nationwide chain's office in your destination city since nearly all reservations are handled by a central reservations office. However, I have been quoted different rates and learned about special offers by talking with several reservationists at the same central reservations office.

Needless to say, it also pays to shop among rental car companies. There are at least a dozen national companies and all maintain toll-free telephone numbers.

Another tip: Many cities, counties, or airport jurisdictions impose high user fees on car rentals. The taxes—often as high as eighteen or twenty percent—can sometimes be avoided by checking the Yellow Pages for your destination city and phoning independent rental car companies at off-airport sites. These savings add up, especially on weekly rates.

I have saved as much as half the cost of my trip by shopping for air, hotel and rental car reservations this way.

27

Travelers Checks and Foreign Exchange

You shouldn't have to pay a fee to purchase travelers checks. Shop around. Many banks, savings banks and credit unions provide travelers checks free to their preferred customers. Also, at the time of this printing, most American Automobile Association (AAA) members receive no-fee travelers checks as a benefit. When traveling outside the U.S., it is advisable to carry travelers checks in a widely-accepted foreign currency, such as the Euro or Japanese yen. Often, these can be obtained without a fee.

Also, when you travel outside the U.S., try to charge as many expenses as possible to your bank credit card. Ordinarily, you will receive the best exchange rate for bank credit card transactions. When traveling abroad, I charge hotel rooms, meals, shopping purchases and almost everything I can to my VISA or American Express card. Invariably, when I receive my monthly statement, I find that the exchange rate is better than any I saw posted in banks or currency exchanges while abroad.

Many credit card issuers have added a two percent or greater surcharge to purchases made abroad. It's important to shop around among credit card companies for the best rates on foreign exchange if you intend to use plastic.

The worst exchange rates are to be found in airports and in currency exchange kiosks on the street, especially those which remain open nights and weekends. If you need cash, the least expensive transactions are made at a major bank during regular business hours. Change U.S. dollar travelers checks into the currency of the foreign country. Exchange enough money to last perhaps a week, since transactions for small amounts often are more costly.

Another tip: Always carry a supply of U.S. $1 bills for gratuities. If you need assistance in an airport or railroad station, a few dollar bills will come in handy.

28

Vacation Check List

Preparing to take a vacation can pose a major challenge. To keep us from forgetting things, my wife and I developed a travel check list. The master copy stays on our computer hard drive, so additions and changes can easily be made. A paper hard copy is kept in a file drawer in case the computer crashes. After about five years of refinement, we have almost everything covered.

At the top of our list is a "90-days prior to departure" heading, which includes such items as making travel reservations, booking lodging, checking passport expiration and setting up a detailed trip itinerary on our computer. A "30-days prior" heading includes securing necessary maps, arranging for house plant watering and most important: paying some of our monthly bills in advance. A "7-days prior" list includes lining up our medications, vitamins and food supplements which we'll be taking along, notifying friends, neighbors and others who need to know, canceling delivery of the newspaper and requesting a "vacation hold" on our mail. Also, we sometimes prepare a list of TV shows to record while we're away.

Our "three-days prior" heading includes cleaning out the refrigerator, checking to make sure all luggage is tagged, and starting to pack. Our "don't forget" list for items to take on the trip is also important. Finally, a "Departure Day" heading includes items such as setting the "toll-saver" switch on our telephone answering machine, pulling the plug on the garage door opener and installing padlocks on the garage door track, moving the hot water heater thermostat control to "vacation" setting, pouring a small amount of bleach into the toilet and turning off its water supply valve. You also may wish to set the heating or air-conditioning control to a "vacation" position.

Since we've begun using this list, we seldom find that we've forgotten anything. And though it's customized for our personal use, many friends have asked for a copy.

29

$mall Town $avings

One of the best-kept secrets in interstate travel is saving money by stopping overnight in or near small towns. Consider this example: My wife and I were driving from Tucson, Arizona, to Sister Bay, Wisconsin. It was late afternoon and we were approaching Kansas City, Missouri. I checked the AAA tour book and noted that rates at many of the recommended motels in Kansas City ranged from $85.00 to $110.00 per night. I also discovered a listing for a rated motel with comparable facilities in Cameron, Missouri, about an hour's drive farther north on our route.

The motel was affiliated with a reputable chain and was just 100 yards from the interstate highway ramp. The motel's published rate was a stunning $48.00 a night. The room turned out to be as well maintained—or better—than some of the big-city rooms we have stayed in at more than double the price. Even better, no big-city parking problems, concerns about "safe" neighborhoods and downtown traffic noise.

Several "mom and pop" restaurants, offering real home cooking, were situated within a mile of the motel. Not only did we book a reservation at the motel for our return trip, but also made sure in the future to look for overnight lodging outside major cities. This approach can also work for you if you're traveling by air and want to avoid paying high room rates in premium cities such as San Francisco, New York, Washington, or Boston. Consider booking in neighboring cities and towns and using public transport to access the big city.

3🔄

Own an Old Car, Rent a New Car

Most of us rent a car when we fly to a destination far from home. However, I learned from my son, Rick, that it's smart to rent a car rather than drive your own even for short pleasure trips or weekend getaways close to home.

Consider this: If your own car, no matter its age or condition, breaks down on the highway, it will have to be towed to the nearest garage or car dealership for repair. Even the most generous American Automobile Association plans don't cover all towing expenses. Last summer, some friends suffered a major transmission breakdown several hundred miles from home. Because repair facilities were inadequate in the nearest town, they had to pay the bill for a tow truck to return their car to the dealership where they live, an expense of $600.00.

If your car breaks down far from home, you're not positioned to shop around for the best deal on repairs, lodging and food. And sometimes, you'll wait several days for needed parts to arrive.

My son says, "Dad, if you're in a rental car and it breaks down, it's somebody else's problem. You just phone the rental car company and they bring you another car and you're on your way."

P.S. Most rental car companies offer attractive special weekend rates, which often start at noon on Thursday and remain in effect until noon on Monday. Many companies offer unlimited miles, but be sure to ask before signing a contract.

31

Don't Leave Home Without It— A Reservation

After an unpleasant experience a few years ago, I swore that I would never again travel without a room reservation.

I was driving alone from California to Wisconsin on highways crowded with summer vacationers. One night about sunset, I pulled off the interstate at a huge motel complex in northern Utah, only to observe a "No Vacancy" sign. Miles later, after passing dozens more such signs, I reached Laramie, Wyoming. It was near midnight, and I could hardly keep my eyes open. A sympathetic innkeeper, whose motel was also booked to capacity, made several phone calls on my behalf. He discovered there wasn't a room to be had anywhere in the state that night. I climbed back in my car and continued driving. At about 3 a.m., exhausted, I stopped for a while at a roadside rest area to snooze, but I soon moved on for fear of becoming a crime victim.

Fighting drowsiness and fatigue, I arrived in Cheyenne at seven the next morning and waited in the lobby of a motel for the first guest to check out and the vacated room to be cleaned. I slept the rest of that day and night. It was the last time I remember traveling without a reservation.

Sometimes a room I've reserved by phone turns out to be one I wouldn't have chosen had I been able to inspect it. But even then, there's an advantage to holding a reservation. Suppose when you arrive at the hotel or motel and when you look around, you are disappointed. Don't go inside. Don't register immediately.

Instead, make some phone calls to check room rates and availability nearby. Visit another lodging facility, and if it's an improvement over what you have reserved, ask the clerk to hold it for you for five minutes. Then call the motel where you hold the reservation and cancel it.

Ordinarily, a motel or hotel will permit you to cancel without penalty. But if you have guaranteed the room by using your credit card and the hotel or motel wants to hold you to the rules, you may have to pay for the unused room, even if you don't occupy it. Either way, you'll have a room for the night. When you make a reservation, always ask about the hotel's cancellation policy.

32

Fly Off-Peak

If you are tired of battling fully-booked flights and crowded airports, you might consider flying when fewer travelers do.

I've found that Saturdays, evenings and holidays are less busy travel times. Whenever possible, my wife and I book our flights on Saturday evenings. Airports are often nearly deserted then and on the plane there's extra room to stretch out in coach class.

Since only snacks or beverages are now served on most flights, we carry on a gourmet picnic and enjoy a leisurely supper en route.

Other days that are also less heavily traveled are holidays, especially Christmas Day and New Year's Day.

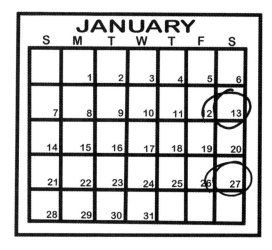

33

Put Your Toilet on 'Vacation Hold'

This isn't funny! The simplest of precautions can save you a deluge of grief. Never leave home after flushing the toilet until you hear the refill mechanism shut off.

I've heard many woeful tales from people who have flushed the toilet, then immediately left their home and headed for work—or worse yet—on vacation. You know the rest.

The toilet mechanism sticks in the open position and when the residents return they find the house flooded—and later receive a water bill that exceeds their monthly rent or mortgage payment.

Recently, friends of ours discovered upon returning from vacation that their ceramic toilet tank had cracked, apparently from old age, during their absence.

Since they hadn't turned off the toilet's water line shutoff valve before departing, the mechanism dutifully kept refilling the tank as water seeped through the tiny crack and onto the floor. The tank refilled automatically every few minutes—for five straight weeks!

34

You're Supposed to Know

When you follow a map toward your intended destination, but reach a fork in the road where it's impossible to make an intelligent choice with the information at hand, what do you do? No signs. No warnings. Well, you're *supposed to know*. If I had the power to create a special Dante's Inferno it would be exclusively for public transportation officials whose insensitivity to the needs of others is responsible for such lack of signs where they are badly needed. It seems to happen to me more often than I'd like.

I'm driving on an unfamiliar stretch of interstate highway and the sign cautioning me that my exit is ahead comes when it's too late for me to change lanes and catch my exit. Or a failure to post a cautionary road sign results in my lining up in the wrong lane when there's a three-lane directional split ahead. I would like to have back the time that's wasted returning to the interstate and starting all over again. I always assume when I encounter a lack of signs that the responsible party simply figured that drivers are *supposed to know*.

One of my all-time favorite examples of this is an expressway exit sign in our city which reads, "Alvernon N.B." A Canadian winter tourist might guess that it means Alvernon, New Brunswick, but locals know that the sign means Alvernon Way, Northbound.

While there's no foolproof solution for avoiding these pitfalls, I find that it helps to request advance detailed driving directions from whomever you're going to call on or visit.

Relationships

35

Looking for the Right One

If you are a man seeking a mate and you would like to find someone who's caring and would be a good mother to your children, avoid a woman whose makeup and hair are always picture-book perfect and who glues on extra-long fingernails.

If you are a woman in search of a man who'll make you a loving husband and be a responsible father and you observe that he mistreats animals or pets, or goes to pieces if he detects a scratch or smudge on the finish of his freshly-waxed sports car, it's a good bet that he's not for you.

A friend of my wife's was married to a man who turned heads. The woman confided to my wife, "Handsome isn't everything—if I were sick in bed, I'd have to crawl to the refrigerator to get myself something to eat."

Long after the honeymoon, when appearances take on reduced importance, you will find that a caring, empathetic spouse manifesting kindness and strength of character is the truly wonderful mate. Beauty is only skin deep, an observation bolstered by the conduct of most egocentric individuals.

Oh, but the person in question might change, you say? That adage about the leopard never changing his spots applies to humans as well. I've seen only one or two exceptions where someone has truly changed. If that's what you're counting on, it's a longshot at best.

36

'Quality Questions'

Questions asked by a person you've just met are a valuable indicator in determining whether he or she is likely to become a friend or a significant other. If the new acquaintance asks what I call "quality questions," it's a good sign that a close relationship is possible. Examples: "What are you reading these days?" "Do you find satisfaction in your work?" "What kinds of things are important to you?"

During a period of years when I was single, I was often disheartened after a first date. The woman might have been pleasant and the evening entertaining, but there was no display of interest in me or my background. I suppose being a journalist and accustomed to asking lots of questions (including personal ones), I found it extraordinary that someone wouldn't want to know where I lived, what I did for work and whether I had children, was divorced, liked to travel, or had a dog.

I vividly recall such a disappointing dating experience. One evening I invited a woman I had met in a hiking club to attend a symphony concert. We talked en route to the concert, and afterwards went for waffles and talked for an hour or more. When I returned home, I realized that this woman, though sociable and polite, had not asked me *one question* during the entire evening. In contrast, when I met my wife, she wanted to know everything about me, and I about her. It didn't take me long to realize that I had met my life partner.

37

Listen Before You Leap

A key consideration in choosing a marriage partner is whether he or she is a person with whom you enjoy talking.

Do you always have something to say to each other? That's especially important as you grow older and superficial attractions diminish. Ask your parents or grandparents if this isn't true.

Unfortunately, too often I've heard a man say, "I married her because she had great legs." Or a woman will admit, "I fell for him because he drove a cute, little red sports car." Well, cars come and go, and so do physical attributes.

Solid, lasting marriages are those in which the partners have many interests in common and enjoy sharing them with each other.

When my wife and I go out to dinner, we see couples who sit through an entire meal in silence. Strange? Well, maybe she once had great legs, and 20 years ago he drove a sporty car. But they're not doing much talking now.

38

How to Ask for a Date

Do you find it difficult to ask for a date? Starting in my teenage years, it was always an ordeal for me to pick up the phone and ask a girl for a date. When I finally got up my nerve, I'd rehearsed dozens of times, but still feared being turned down. My anxiety continued well into my adult years, and it wasn't until a friend shared this secret with me that I finally shed my fears.

This is what he told me: "Look, George. You pick up the phone and you call, saying 'I have tickets for a concert in San Francisco next Saturday evening and, I'd like to invite you to join me.' That's all you need to say. No hemming or hawing. Just that. Nothing more!"

The next day I decided to try it and phoned a woman to whom I had been recently introduced. It worked! From that day forward, I was no longer inhibited. Of course, I was turned down from time to time. But, who isn't? Do ball players have 1.000 batting averages? Do salesmen write up an order at every door they knock on? Why should asking for a date be different? This approach worked for me, and it's worked for many others with whom I've shared it.

Oh, I must confess…I didn't always have tickets for the event. I waited to buy them until the date offer was accepted. But, I always checked with the box office about ticket availability just before making my call for a date.

39

Two Books That Will Change Your Life

When I'm asked to recommend books for self-improvement, I never hesitate to respond because the two books that I consider most valuable are classics and have been reprinted dozens of times. They are *The Art of Loving* by Erich Fromm and *How to Win Friends and Influence People* by Dale Carnegie.

Fromm's work will help you to understand what's needed to establish a lasting relationship. Carnegie's book offers tips on how to get along with others. If you take to heart what the authors offer, you assuredly will benefit.

P.S. If you wish to add another timeless title to your list, read *Walden Two* by B. F. Skinner. Although considered a utopian novel, it provides the best explanation for human behavior in a form that's easy to understand. All these titles are available in paperback. You should be able to find copies in bookstores, used bookstores or public libraries.

40

'The Man in the Green Hat'

Jacque Fresco, the man to whom this book is dedicated, taught me how to pose delicate questions. He termed it "the man in the green hat" strategy.

Example: You are seated at a table in a restaurant with a woman you recently met and like very much. You would like to know how she feels about someone who has been married and divorced twice, but you aren't ready to reveal that you're talking about yourself. So, instead, you point to a man a few tables away and say, "You see that man in the green hat over there? I once worked with him. He's a super guy, but he's been married and divorced twice."

You are likely get an honest reaction from her because it's not *you* who's being assessed. It's the man in the green hat. That's safe.

Your companion might react, saying, "That's terrible. I would never want to get involved with a person who's been married and divorced twice." Hearing that might end the relationship, but at least you know how she really feels about this question.

The "man in the green hat" technique can be a very effective and non-threatening method for soliciting feedback on sensitive issues that you don't want to confront head-on.

41

Raising Kids

Thousands of books have been published on this subject. I'm no expert, but I want to share a couple of observations.

I'm a parent myself and I'm intrigued with the reasons some kids turn out okay and others don't. I've heard many experts lecture on the subject and I've read a good amount. But I seldom have seen *responsibility* given enough emphasis. I'm talking about giving children age-appropriate responsibilities starting at age three or four and continuing as long as they live under your roof. A century ago, when more families lived on farms, every youngster was expected to do chores.

Today, with most of us living in urban or suburban settings, kids grow up in townhouses, apartments, or condos and can't be sent outside to weed, hoe, mow or milk.

However, urban parents can make it a priority to assign household chores within their children's range of capability. These might include picking up and storing toys, helping in the kitchen, folding laundry or washing the family car.

Cash allowances should be earned, rather than seen as entitlements. Children should be frequently lauded for their efforts—the more positive reinforcement the better.

When you teach children at a young age to take responsibility, you also introduce them to taking responsibility for their actions. They can learn from you the elements that go into good decision-making. These will someday lead them into how to prepare for making important life choices. Youngsters who have learned how to make decisions independently are less likely to be followers.

Encourage participation in extracurricular school activities, part-time jobs and, above all, any sign of initiative or enterprise. Hand-fed kids are not prepared to face the challenges of today's world. You can make the difference.

Life Skills

42

Find the Expert

For everything and for every problem there's an expert. The challenge is to find that person.

People needing cataract surgery should seek out an eye surgeon who's done thousands of cataract operations. You don't want the surgeon fresh out of residency.

My wife once bought a painting for fifty cents at a thrift store, and it took us six months to find an expert who identified it as the work of a well-known Canadian artist active in the 1940s and 1950s.

There are many other experts. If, for example, you have a farm that you want to trade for shares in a limited partnership in some offshore oil rigs, there is someone at the IRS who can answer your accountant's most detailed questions about tax consequences in this specific area.

There are medical experts around the world who have based their careers on the study of one particular disease or disorder and are widely published in professional journals. These are the experts you or your physician may need to contact.

It's not commonly known, but there are databases of experts in various fields. However, you need to know where to look. One place to start is the Internet, using a powerful search engine—my favorite is Google.

Suppose you are looking for someone to authenticate an autographed baseball signed "Babe Ruth." You would enter the following into the search engine: "Babe Ruth" AND "autographed baseball." If your search brings up a large number of references, you might narrow your search by entering "Babe Ruth" AND "autographed baseball" AND "expert."

From there, it's a matter of sifting through a list of names you've collected, followed up by phone calls. In the end, if you've done your homework, you'll have a qualified expert to render an opinion on the autograph.

When it counts, I always seek the expert.

43

Keep Informed

A shocking number of Americans are grossly uninformed about what goes on in their community, their nation and the world. Fewer young people subscribe to a daily newspaper; they get their news from television.

However, you'll find that among people who enjoy a high standard of living, virtually *all* subscribe to a daily newspaper, often more than one. They know that it's absolutely necessary to keep up with the latest developments everywhere.

Those who don't won't learn about major changes in the economy, retirement funding, the local real estate market, health care, technology, travel or the environment. And those who don't have access to the Internet are also at a disadvantage.

It's equally important to know how to use the Internet's search engines. Whether you're seeking a job, checking out a particular pharmaceutical or making travel plans, the search engines will provide you with virtually every detail available.

Ten years ago the Internet was not a part of our lives. Today, the lives of my wife and myself often depend on the Internet.

44

Don't Ask Twice Ask Three Times

Have you noticed that the quality of service is slipping and errors have become a way of life?

A case in point: Recently, I needed some equipment for my computer printer. I phoned the authorized local dealer only to be informed they were out of stock and that the item was no longer being made. A call to the manufacturer's warehouse, however, disclosed that the equipment was indeed still available, though in limited quantity. Three days later, the item was delivered. Similar experiences are an everyday occurrence in my life.

It was my wife's cousin, who introduced us to the "Ask three times" rule. It pays off when asking directions, checking prices and in hundreds of other situations when you can't rely on the first answer you receive. Try it!

45

Defensive Driving

When I was a cub reporter covering police, I attended a news conference at which the county's sheriff emphasized the importance of defensive driving. His reasoning: "You must assume that everyone driving out there is an idiot and is going to do the wrong thing almost every time."

The sheriff gave an example. A motorist preparing to turn left at an intersection shouldn't take for granted that a car signaling a left turn from the opposite direction will actually turn. If that driver decides to continue straight ahead at the last moment, the left-turning motorist is in big trouble. Wait until the other vehicle actually begins making the signaled turn, the sheriff emphasized, adding that a defensive driver would always assume that the other driver was going to do something other than the signaled action.

Two other sound driving tips: (1) When followed by a tailgater, pull over to the side and let the other vehicle pass; (2) Stay behind the vehicle ahead of you a distance of one car length for every 10 miles per hour of speed.

Defensive driving should become automatic, like driving itself.

46

The Power of "Thank You"

A "Thank-You" card or letter can pay huge dividends, especially in these times when expressions of gratitude are on the decline. "Thank-You" notes have landed me a job, cut through red tape, secured needed approval for something—or brought just plain appreciation.

A particular experience comes to mind. I had been invited to a New Year's Eve party by a young woman with whom I was acquainted through a hiking club. I was unmarried at the time and had no plans for New Year's Eve. So, when I received a phone call inviting me to attend her party, I gratefully accepted although I was virtually a stranger to the hostess and her guests.

The party was pleasant, but uneventful and I departed shortly after the New Year was ushered in. The next day, I routinely mailed a "Thank-You" card to the hostess, mentioning that I had had an enjoyable evening.

Several weeks later, I encountered the hostess in the supermarket. After a few words of small talk, the young woman mentioned my card, confiding that it was the first "Thank-you" card she'd ever received.

I was dumbfounded. This woman was in her early thirties, educated, a professional woman—and this was the first time in her life that she had received a written expression of thanks? It caused me to realize the importance of a "Thank-You" card and the impact that it can make.

Another memorable experience came after I had given a brief tour of Miami to a visiting minor official at the request of my boss. After the visitor returned home, I received a letter which I have kept. Typed on his official letterhead were these words: "Thanks, George. I hope I can be so kind to you sometime." The entire body of the letter consisted of only that one line of type.

That single line really stood out, and the example has served me well. I have used that same message for my own "Thank-You" letters numerous times. "Thank you" in writing requires so little. It sets you apart from others. It can be one of the best investments you'll ever make.

47

How to Play the Game

In pursuing an important objective, it is vital to know everything you can about what you will encounter—both on the stage as well as behind the scenes.

If you are considering opening a business in a small community, consult someone who knows that community well and who can tell you whose blessing you require and how to get it. Our government operates the Central Intelligence Agency to provide high-level officials with such information (forget those CIA intrigues—they make good movie plots) so that they don't walk completely cold into potentially sticky situations. You can do the same.

I knew a developer who wanted to build an attractive office park in a California suburb known for its opposition to growth. The first thing he did was hire an environmentally-sensitive public relations firm to produce a preliminary report informing him of the various obstacles he would encounter along with advice on how to overcome them.

On another occasion, a family I knew brought their aged and sick father here from a foreign country where he had been living alone. They were unable to obtain immigration approval, so in desperation he came here on a tourist visa. After several months, when his visa expired, immigration officials sent a notice ordering that he return to his native country. His family pleaded for an exception due to his age, illness and the fact that there was no one in his homeland to care for him. The request was denied. The family contacted a young immigration attorney they found in the Yellow Pages.

He agreed to take the case and appeal the decision though pointing out that his fees and court costs could run as high as $10,000 to $15,000 and that success wasn't assured.

I subsequently referred the family to another immigration attorney, a more seasoned practitioner, who after being briefed, recommended that the family do nothing. Yes, *do nothing*. The attorney explained that he was familiar with the operation of the regional office from where the immigration notice had been mailed. He said he had firsthand knowledge that the office was grossly understaffed and inundated with cases and likely would not get around to taking any action for months, if not years.

That attorney knew what he was talking about. The family received no further communications about the pending matter. Four years later, the father died peacefully at his daughter and son-in-law's home at the age of 92, his loved ones at his bedside.

48

When to Give Advice

Have you noticed that very few people accept advice? I'm unable to count the times that my wife and I have had our advice spurned by neighbors, friends and relatives who imply through their actions, "Thanks, but we know what we're doing." We've discovered that when most people ask for advice, they're really looking for validation.

While working in California, I once found myself among a group of reporters awaiting a major announcement from a press spokesman. During our bull session, the conversation turned to tales about a well-known editor of a big city newspaper and why he was successful.

An old-timer in the group spoke up and offered this explanation: He described the editor as an exception to the above-mentioned phenomenon and explained he was successful because he knew he was no genius but was smart enough to hire people who knew more than he did. Once hired, he relied upon them for their advice and expertise. It's clear that most of the truly great leaders surround themselves with brilliant advisers, aides and deputies, then draw on their experience.

If you're not willing to learn from the experience of others, you have only your own limited ones to benefit from. That's doing it the hard way.

49

Hardship or Opportunity?

One of the most important things I wish I'd known earlier in life is the satisfaction of making someone else happy. When I was young, I was willing to help, give, care or listen, but I considered it a sacrifice. I felt that by giving to others I was somehow diminishing my own welfare. Thankfully, as I matured, that attitude changed.

When I was a newspaper reporter, I interviewed a prominent local attorney who had recently been elected president of the state bar. In the course of the interview, I asked him whether the duties of the new job would impose a hardship on his law practice. The attorney, who was nearing retirement age, seemed surprised at my question.

"Why, no," he replied. "I never considered it a hardship. This is an opportunity for *service*."

It would be still a few more years before I fully understood what he meant. At some point, I came to realize that all the tangibles we acquire in life—luxuries, gadgets, wealth—pale in comparison to the inner satisfaction that comes when you help another human being. And no one really needs to tell me "thank you." The satisfaction is intrinsic. In your heart *you* know what you've done and that's enough.

50

Who's Your Mentor?

When I see the "Got milk?" ads, I always think they should instead say, "Got a mentor?"

Looking back at decisions I've made or something I've written or said to others when I was younger, I often cringe. "Did I really say that?" I ask myself. "How could I have been so naive or foolish?"

Now, reflecting on those early years, I realize how much I could have benefited from having a mentor. But, I didn't have one, and I had to rely on my peers for advice—usually young people as immature and self-centered as I was.

If you are in your twenties or thirties or even older, try to find someone with a lot of life experience and perhaps some sagacity who is willing to help you with your problems and help you grow as a person. Your mentor has likely "seen the movie before," so to speak, and can help by talking over things with you. Facing a big decision in your life? Get your mentor's take on the situation before you make up your mind.

51

When to Act Quickly

As incomprehensible as it may seem, most people are reluctant to act quickly at the first sign that something is awry. Studies show that people continue sitting in a medical office waiting room thumbing through magazines while puffs of smoke in plain sight billow from a vent in the same room. No one takes any action. No one wants to stand out from the crowd.

Those who do are the exception, and hopefully, that includes you. To be the exception, one must develop a mental acuity that senses danger and acts quickly. If you're in an unfamiliar city and find you've inadvertently entered what appears to be a high-crime neighborhood, waste no time in leaving. If you're lost, watch for a police car, a service station or a convenience market to ask directions. If you're in a restaurant or bar and some customers become unruly, pay your tab and leave. Don't wait for bottles to start flying.

Being alert for signs of trouble and responding quickly can spare you emotional distress, too. Suppose you're among colleagues at work or family members or friends who are disputing a sensitive issue. Your antennae tell you that this situation is explosive and you're bound to be drawn into the fray. Make any excuse and head for the door. This is not to say that you should cut and run when your departmental budget needs defending. But, why get into it with your mother-in-law for the 143rd time? Surely, you should have learned from previous encounters when a situation is futile.

52

Hire the Best

It doesn't really cost any more to hire the best.

Good examples are attorneys, including those specializing in divorce, taxes or probate. With the exception of such locations as New York and Washington, D.C., most first-class lawyers bill at rates ranging from $250 to $400 per hour. Many small-town or less-experienced lawyers bill at $175 to $250 per hour, seldom lower.

Most top-of-the-line attorneys not only keep up to date on the latest changes and developments in their specialized fields, but also are fully familiar with the internal workings of various government offices that relate to their practice. For example, such an attorney might suggest, "Let's wait until next week to file our papers because Mr. A. will be back from vacation and he isn't as tough on new applicants as Mr. B., who will be away on temporary assignment then."

I was fortunate once to consult a lawyer who kept abreast of real estate tax legislation to the extent that he received a daily report from Capitol Hill as to what a House committee was considering in connection with a measure to change laws governing the tax-free exchange of real property. He was in a position to advise me on a subject on that particular day when most other lawyers or accountants couldn't do so because they lacked that same information—information that would subsequently pass into their hands later, but too late for me.

Also, when you hire the best within a certain specialty, they often are accorded privileges that the average practitioner doesn't enjoy. This applies in medicine as well. Not long ago, I contacted a medical specialist while seeking information on behalf of a relative. In a half hour, the specialist phoned me back saying, "I just talked to one of the top experts in the country at Massachusetts General Hospital and he told me that as of this moment there have been no new advances in the treatment of this disorder."

You'll also find that in any community the best know the best. This is true in virtually all fields. It seems that the best tax lawyer can direct you to the best immigration lawyer and the best primary care physician can tell you who is the best surgeon.

There's a handyman in our city—let's call him Jack—who charges only slightly more than other handymen. We use his services for almost everything and my wife always says, "If you hire Jack, you pay a little bit more, but you only have to pay him once. He does the job right the first time."

Overall, my rule is if the issue impacts on your health, your family or your finances, settle for no one but the best person in that field. It's not the time to bargain hunt.

53

Everyone Needs a 'Board of Directors'

Individuals need a "board of directors" as much as any corporation. Why? Because we know that several heads are better than one when it comes to making important decisions.

This doesn't mean that your board will make your decisions for you, but, the members will provide you with their advice. Of course, the final decision is yours.

Who sits on an individual's board? The friends and relatives you think will give you the best advice. Ordinarily, there are no formal appointments and no formal meetings. And most often the word "board" is not even used.

You are responsible for convening your advisors if and when the need arises. Usually, you confer one-on-one, often on the phone. It's likely that your advisers don't see themselves as members of a formal "board," but rather as friends helping friends.

When I have a major medical or financial decision pending, I inform the professional or service provider that I must consult with my "board of directors." Normally, the process requires not more than 24 to 48 hours.

This approach to decision-making is a two-way street. I also serve on the boards of many of those who serve on mine.

54

Best Evening to Dine Out

It's well known that Friday and Saturday nights are a restaurant's busiest because that's when most people go out. But Monday and Tuesday, which are the least busy days, have their drawbacks, too. Some restaurants are closed on Monday and Tuesday because business is slow on those evenings.

According to an expert who was in the restaurant business for many years, the best evening to dine out is Thursday. The principal players—the owner, chef and top servers—will be on duty gearing up for a busy weekend. So, you'll have a better chance of getting good food and attentive service, and there won't be a line of customers waiting for your table.

55

Hard-to-Find Items

When you find a great pair of shoes or the best pruning shears in the world—or any other item that you'd like to use for years to come—and it comes time to reorder, what do you do?

You go back to where you bought the item only to be informed that the manufacturer has discontinued it or the store no longer stocks the item. Or maybe you've been searching for something that you've been wanting to buy and no one seems to offer it.

Well, you need be disappointed no more. You can now use the Internet to help you find it, and the chances are great that you will find it.

I've used Internet searches to locate, among other things, matching replacement hinges for an old door, a discontinued replacement part for a telephone headset and a VHS recording of a pre-1980s TV drama, all of which I was informed were no longer obtainable.

Often neighbors, relatives and friends contact us to search the Internet for them when they can't find a needed product or item.

We start by using the Google search engine and go from there. What's most important are the search words you choose to enter. It might seem difficult at first, but you'll find that your searching techniques will improve over time.

In the last year, we located a Norwegian hand cream and a special brand of canned pea soup for a neighbor who had all but given up searching. However, the most satisfying find was a mechanical oven timer/clock for our stove. The original one had lived its life of twenty years and couldn't be repaired. However, the stove and oven were still working just fine and we weren't ready to buy a new one.

Our handyman was informed by his supplier that the part was no longer available through the manufacturer. Using the Internet and phone contacts, we learned that the manufacturer had cleared out the old replacement parts after twenty years and sold them in bulk to a bidder. It turned out that the bidder stored them on his farm in South Carolina. When our handyman phoned, the man answered and said he would need to go out to his barn to check to see if he had the requested part. After a wait, he returned saying he did and subsequently shipped us a factory-new replacement timer/clock.

If you can't find the product or item using Google, and you're willing to accept a used or resale item, try entering the item in the eBay search engine. If the item is for sale anywhere in the world, it will often show up in the eBay search.

And if you're looking for a hard-to-find or out-of-print book, try doing a search at either abebooks.com or alibris.com. These websites list millions of titles both new and used.

56

Build a Support Base

If you've ever heard, "Sorry, but we can't get to you for three weeks," when you need an appointment for services, you'll know why it's wise to maintain a cadre of professionals and tradespeople on whom you can rely. However, forming a support base requires an investment of both your time and your loyalty. That's because life is a two-way street.

First, through trial and error I find people who do good work at reasonable prices. Once I've found them, I stop shopping around. I figure that if their prices are fair, their loyalty is worth far more than the pennies I might occasionally shave off by shopping. I seldom question their prices unless I need their estimate for a large job. Then, I simply ask, "What cost range are we looking at?"

Besides receiving good work at fair prices, the biggest payoff comes when you phone with an urgent need and the response comes back, "We're awfully busy, but we'll find some way to work you in."

57

Update Your Priorities

How often have you seen people throw up their hands in frustration when their plans get interrupted? If you're a busy person juggling several projects at once, you'll need to reorder your priorities continuously. There's no way to avoid it because unexpected demands for your time will rise from nowhere. And, of course, many of these new demands will be important, if not critical.

I've worked with individuals who are competent, but can't seem to get comfortable with the notion that they can't stick to their planned schedules come hell or high water. Once I stood in line at an independently-owned quick-printing facility and watched an employee reject a 5,000-piece printing job because "We're just too busy to take it right now." At the time he was running a dozen photocopies for a customer and had a few more small jobs pending.

Wow, I thought to myself, I can only guess how the owner might have reacted had he been there at the time.

As a youngster, planning my day was relatively simple. There was a list of "must-do" household chores, homework and a wide choice of recreational options such as playing sandlot baseball, watching television or riding my bicycle. Gradually, the list began to expand and, as it did, making choices became more difficult. By the time I reached young adulthood, I sometimes felt overwhelmed by the size and scope of my list. For example, I would begin work on a particular project for my boss, only to be buzzed by another department head who needed me to get busy on a project for him.

Then I came across an article titled "Ordering and Reordering Your Personal Priorities." The gist of the article was that we must rank our priorities at the beginning of each day and then accept the fact that it might be necessary to reorder them again or even several more times during the day.

Now, I keep a "to do" list on my desk calendar. Tasks that I don't get done one week are moved to the next week. I never accomplish all my tasks, so many are carried over for several weeks. There are even some tasks, such as cleaning out the garage, which have been carried over for months.

Often, people complain that they feel pressured by their lists of uncompleted tasks. My advice is this: Do the *most important* tasks first and tackle the others as time allows.

You can't have the cleanest house, be the best gardener, play piano at concert level, make the most money and be an outstanding volunteer all in the same 24-hour day. In short, you can't do everything.

We must learn to choose carefully and accept that some aspirations will have to be set aside. At the same time, we must remain flexible and exercise the good judgment to know when it's appropriate to make an instant switch in our plans and when to stay the course.

58

Many Eggs, Many Baskets

The saying about not putting all your eggs in one basket is as valid now as when it was sparkling new.

One of the biggest mistakes people make is to rely on a single source—one person for happiness or, as a business person, one source for goods and services.

It's wise to have one or several backup sources, whether in your professional or personal life.

59

Beyond Financial Success

Many of us find satisfaction in helping those in need. We work through religious organizations, make cash contributions or perform community service. Without such personal giving our society would be poorer, indeed. Some people, who have given their share during their lifetime, feel that perhaps they could do more. They are moderately affluent and through wills or living trusts, have bequeathed substantial amounts to worthwhile causes.

But, why wait until after you're gone? Why not put some of that money to use while you can have the satisfaction of seeing the results of your generosity?

Public examples who immediately come to mind are CNN founder Ted Turner and financier George Soros, both of whom have contributed millions to worthwhile causes during their lifetimes. However, you don't have to be a millionaire to help furnish a room in a home for battered women, send a needy kid to summer camp or dedicate a small park or playground in memory of a loved one. You can endow a scholarship program or fund an annual volunteer award. Such opportunities abound in every community.

Remember, wealth is only a scorecard. The wise and generous use of your financial assets can be a source of deep, inner satisfaction.

60

Once a Bum, Always a Bum

Many years ago, when my son and I joined a fantasy baseball league, I vividly remember a novice participant using his precious first round draft pick to select a veteran player who had a reputation for controversy. When he named his choice, a more experienced league member chided him for making the selection, saying of the controversial player: "Once a bum, always a bum!" The novice defended his selection, saying he believed his player might turn over a new leaf in the season ahead.

As it turned out, the "once a bum" pronouncement was accurate. The player spent more than half the season either on the bench or under suspension and was of little value to our fellow league member.

Since this incident, I've made it a point to observe similar situations in real life. Guess what? Our veteran league member was right.

In my experience, I've seldom known of a mature person to change his behavior or personality. Believing this, I applied the knowledge by putting it into practice in my everyday decisions. But I once made an exception. I accepted a renter who had a poor credit history but assured me that he had changed his habits. His appeal convinced me. In the end it turned out that his behavior had *not* changed and my experience with him was considerably less than satisfactory.

I suppose there are some people who have truly changed their ways. However, to date, I haven't met one.

61

College—When?

If you're a parent and have kids who are approaching college age, you might want to consider some collected wisdom on the question of who should go to college and *when*. As a one-time college dropout who later, as a veteran, returned to school, I'm speaking from firsthand experience.

When I was a reporter, I covered a speech by a university dean who emphatically declared that no student should be admitted to college within two years of high school graduation. He said that during those two years, the student should either work in the private sector or enter a government public service program or the military. He believed that young people, immediately out of high school, were not sufficiently mature to fully benefit from a college education.

I was in my thirties when I returned to college, attending evening classes and working full time. It was a totally different experience than when I entered college at age seventeen. This time I was motivated and found most of the classes interesting if not rewarding. I thrived on the challenges posed. If I could turn back the clock, I would have followed the dean's recommendations and first completed my military service, then worked at some jobs before entering college.

I would add to those recommendations that every high school and college student should have a part-time job, either after school, on weekends, or during the summer. It builds character and prepares a young person for a competitive environment.

62

College—Where?

Are you among those who have discovered that bigger isn't always better? I strongly believe that this truism applies to colleges, too.

If you have a son or daughter who is *ready* for the college experience, and I stress *ready* because of what was discussed in the previous chapter, then consider steering them toward a small private college.

One of my regrets is that I did not attend such a college. That isn't to say that one can't get a good education at a large institution, because I did. But that ivy-covered-brick, small college experience was missing, and its benefits can't be overstated.

A freshman at a state university or a two-year community college is a number—one of thousands. She often sits in an auditorium so large that the instructor must use a microphone to lecture to the class. This makes for little possibility of give and take between student and instructor. Sometimes students aren't even in the same classroom as their instructors; they view their class lecture on delayed video while sitting alone in a cubicle. Exams are scored by computer.

In contrast, small private colleges often have enrollments of 1,000 to 2,000 students. I once visited a college in Wisconsin with an enrollment of 1,200. The ratio of instructors to students was approximately one to ten. On campus, students greeted each other by first name. Everyone had a chance to participate in sports, musical performances, dances, homecoming events, hear visiting lecturers and other typical small college functions. It was impossible for a student to be anonymous or get lost in the crowd.

Graduates of small colleges treasure memories of their time there. They maintain contacts with their fellow alumni and their alma maters throughout life. The friendships a student develops during these years are priceless and can open doors, both socially as well as in business and the professions.

An admissions counselor at the college I visited explained that any student applying for admission, who had reasonably good high school grades, would be offered help in the form of a tuition package. The package consisted of work-study funding, a student loan and a partial scholarship. Only a portion of the tuition would be paid by the student's parents. Very few applicants were ever turned down, he said proudly.

While the small private college experience isn't a possibility for everyone, if your child sees the benefit in this experience and really wants to go, you should do all you can to help. I emphasize *help* because I don't believe you do your child a favor by paying the entire expense. The student needs to contribute, too, and will value his or her education even more because of it.

If after graduating, your son or daughter seeks a postgraduate education, that's the time to start looking at larger universities.

63

A 'Road Map' For Everything

When I applied for my first newspaper job, an older friend advised me that I wouldn't be considered for the position unless I was willing to "campaign" for it. He pointed out that the newspaper's editor had a drawer full of applications, many from job seekers more qualified than I.

My friend provided me with a list of things I needed to do to remain in the running. He said I should phone in any news tips I could come up with over the next several weeks and ask contacts known to the editor to write recommendation letters on my behalf.

He also put me in contact with an employee at the newspaper who informed me that the editor never hired anyone who did not come into the office in person at least *three* times after applying—a sign of the applicant's interest and eagerness to work at the newspaper.

Four months later, I received a phone call informing me that I had been hired.

When I thanked my friend and expressed amazement at his knowledge of how to approach the challenge, he responded by telling me, "There's a road map for everything."

64

Hard-to-Get Appointments

Are you surprised when you must sometimes wait two or three months for a medical or dental appointment? Such long waits are becoming commonplace these days, but there's a way to get around it. The same approach will often work for show tickets and dinner reservations. At least, sometimes.

Here's how: The next time you phone for a medical appointment and you're informed that the first one available is in six weeks, take it. Then, immediately ask that your name be placed on the waiting list of patients who wish to be contacted in case of an earlier cancellation. You'll find that about half of the medical offices will respond that they are unable to contact you when there's a cancellation because, because, because.... In which case, you ask if it's okay to check with them periodically. You won't get an enthusiastic "yes," but most office receptionists would be hard put to tell you "no."

Begin calling once a day. Be extra polite and solicitous, even apologetic. If you live or work near their office, make it a point to mention that and that you can drive there within a few minutes. This is a plus because often a patient will cancel on short notice and the office is eager to fill the time slot. Become acquainted with the staff and always ask for the same person. Be complimentary. Thank the person for taking her time to check. At some point, the staff member might even ask for your phone number. In the end, you have a good chance of getting someone's canceled appointment, if for no other reason than the office staff realizes they won't have to answer your daily calls any more.

Recently, I phoned for a medical appointment and learned that the next opening was in three weeks. I booked the date, but went through my spiel anyway. Twenty minutes later, I received a call from the receptionist asking if I could be there in 15 minutes. I scrambled and saw the doctor within an hour of making my first call.

You can apply this same strategy to other hard-to-get appointments as well as tickets and various reservations.

APPOINTMENT

TIME: _2:30 PM_

DATE: _October 2_

65

'Wipe It Off!'

When I coached Little League, the team's manager would often encounter a player who became dejected after striking out or dropping an easy fly ball. "Wipe it off!" he would call out to the youngster.

With few exceptions, the player would quickly recover his composure and again focus on the game. Seeing this undoubtedly left an impression because since then I have admonished myself using the same words whenever I make a bad play, so to speak.

It might be a business setback or receiving a "no" answer to what I thought was a reasonable request.

In such instances, I remind myself to "Wipe it off!" and get back to my business. To dwell on misfortune produces nothing and prevents one from going forward.

66

Avoiding the Rowdies

Picnickers who play booming boom boxes, are intoxicated, or behave in an inconsiderate, raucous, or vulgar manner can ruin your day in the outdoors. However, there's a way you can avoid them.

Place your picnic items into baskets or knapsacks and hike in at least one mile from the parking lot.

Hikers are a different class of folks. They usually don't litter, are most often friendly and considerate, and are protective of the environment. Rowdies tend *not* to be the hiking type.

In more than 30 years of hiking, I've never encountered any rowdies on the trail. They prefer to drive directly to their picnic spots and wouldn't dream of walking even a few hundred yards, much less a couple of miles. Besides that, those beer coolers are heavy.

As for public places such as malls and supermarkets, your chances of avoiding rude and boisterous people are best if you schedule your shopping trips for early morning when the stores first open.

Reason? Such folks are not typically early risers.

Your Health

67

Naps Aren't Just for Babies

My Uncle Max, who began taking afternoon naps at the age of 60, lived in good health to be 93 years old. His advice to me was, "No matter what your age, get off your feet for at least a half-hour every day."

My uncle didn't always sleep, but he stretched out in a reclining chair or on the bed for at least 30 minutes. Uncle Max apparently was on the right track because since then I've read that taking naps reduces the chance of a heart attack by 30 percent.

I've been following my uncle's advice for more than 15 years and I always feel refreshed after a nap. I'm able to work after dinner until ten or eleven o'clock. For me, it's nature's pep pill.

68

When It Pays to Shop

If you move to a new community, you'll need the services of a physician, dentist, auto mechanic, lawyer and bank. Easy enough. But, you shouldn't feel you need to stay with the first provider you find, especially if they don't meet your expectations. The secret is to shop around.

In one city, I went through seven dentists before finding the right one for me. Some service providers are honest, but not competent. Others are competent, but not necessarily honest.

This kind of "shopping" is a screening process, and it takes time. But, it's worth it.

69

Managing Your Health Care

Most people no longer enjoy personalized health care, but have become numbers on an assembly line. This doesn't necessarily mean we should expect poor or substandard care, but it's easy to get lost in the administrative shuffle. I refer to all facets of health care: physicians, dentists, hospitals, nursing homes and, yes, chiefly HMOs (Health Maintenance Organizations).

There are too many instances in which patients fail to receive needed treatment or—the opposite problem—receive unnecessary tests, medication or surgery. This is the result, among other things, of patients being kept in the dark about economic incentives to the provider as well as incompetence, expediency and sloppy record keeping. You can protect yourself by being involved in your own health care.

First, *shop* for medical practitioners and HMOs; ask questions and compare your findings. Meet the care provider and decide whether you'd be comfortable with that provider and how he or she feels about sharing decision-making with you. Try to talk to other people who are patients of that care provider.

In decisions affecting your health care, it helps to know as much as you can about your medical problems. As we all know, a physician's time with a patient is limited. So, you need to be well organized to receive maximum benefit. Get right to the issue. I always first consult *The Merck Manual* and learn as much as I can about my suspected problem or disorder. *The Merck Manual* is an incredible document of more than 2,000 pages and is available at most bookstores. I also go online and search the Internet for additional information.

By the time I reach the physician's office, I have become a mini-authority on the subject and can intelligently converse with my doctor. Ordinarily, I'm sufficiently informed to ask why I'm being put on a certain medication or why I must undergo a test. Many physicians now encourage patients to do their own research on the Internet.

Any time I encounter a serious medical problem, I seek not only a second opinion, but often a third or fourth opinion. By serious, I am referring to any condition where surgery or an invasive procedure is recommended. I also talk to anyone who has any firsthand knowledge about the subject. In addition, there are a number of independent professional researchers who, for a modest fee, will conduct an intensive search of your problem and compile a comprehensive report for you. The search includes various databases, including medical journals, magazines, newspapers and online articles.

Also remember, if you are a patient in a hospital or nursing home, you have a legal right to ask what medication or treatment you are receiving and why. If you don't wish to have the medication or treatment, you can refuse it under the law of informed consent.

In today's changing world, it no longer seems advisable to place yourself totally in the hands of any one person or institution. Ask questions and view the situation as if you were a chairman of the board seeking advice from various experts before making the final decision. After all, it's your life, isn't it?

70

Sleeping Problems

Rather than take medications to get to sleep, I've found four different approaches, all of which seem to work at various times. First, as soon as my head hits the pillow, in my mind I pull down an imaginary stage curtain. Behind that curtain are the normal cares of the day. I tell myself that I must leave unfinished work and concerns until morning, assured that they will all be there when I awake. Further, I remind myself that there's nothing more I can do about them tonight. That done, I begin to visualize—it might be a mountain lake, a sunset or another relaxing setting. Any scene will do, so long as it won't stimulate you or keep you awake.

If I can't get to sleep, I go to the living room and slip into the recliner chair with a book. Don't choose a book that's a page-turner or thriller. A friend told me that it took him 30 years to read Thomas Mann's *The Magic Mountain*. In the same manner, on and off, I've been reading a 600-page biography for more than a year, and I'm seldom able to read more than two or three pages before dozing off. The book is reserved exclusively for this purpose.

A third approach is better used for occasions when I awaken before dawn and can't get back to sleep. When I was working 9 to 5, this would upset me because I reasoned that I needed the extra sleep and wouldn't get it. A colleague suggested that I drink a glass of water, but not eat any food, then return to bed telling myself: "It's okay if I don't get back to sleep. I'll just lie down and rest for another hour until the alarm clock rings."

Yet another approach is to switch on the TV with the volume set low. Often, I'll half-awaken to hear a minute or two of a program, then doze off again.

While none of these approaches can claim 100 percent effectiveness, it's a far cry from earlier days when I would fidget, then get up at 5 or 6 a.m. and declare the day ruined due to lack of sleep.

Though I have no scientific proof, experience causes me to believe that the hours we sleep prior to midnight are more beneficial to us than those after midnight. Translation: If you get your eight hours between 10 p.m. and 6 a.m., you'll feel better than if you sleep from 2 a.m. to 10 a.m.

In support of this notion, I recall when I was working as a police reporter during my early days in journalism, one of my first duties in the morning was to visit the graveyard-shift watch commander at the sheriff's department to review the previous night's reports. I once asked him if it was difficult for him to sleep during the day. His response surprised me. In the twelve years he had been working graveyard, he said, he couldn't recall a single day when he'd had "a good night's sleep."

71

When You Catch a Cold

For as long as I can remember, consumers have been bombarded with cold-remedy advertisements. Many ads suggest that you don't need rest to recover. Just pop a couple of pills and you'll feel like a million dollars. Don't believe it! Many of those highly-advertised cold remedies contain some form of antihistamine which dries up your sinuses and stops a running nose. While these over-the-counter medications may retard or repress your cold symptoms, they *do not cure* the cold. Worse yet, these medications give you a false sense that you are improving.

Instead of going to work and spreading your cold around, you should be home resting, sleeping and drinking lots of fluids. How often have you heard someone complain about being unable to shake a cold or flu for six or eight weeks? Chances are they have been keeping their normal work schedule.

It wasn't until the 1950s, when antihistamines became available over the counter, that folks came to believe that colds or flu could be disregarded by taking a few tablets. My experience has been that if you take care of yourself immediately, you won't need more than a week to completely recover. A nasty flu bug can take longer. If there's fever, you should contact your doctor.

72

Solving by Trial and Error

Ever wonder why you feel bad? Perhaps, you are allergic to something and don't know what it is. Take heart in knowing that in science one of the greatest challenges is the attribution of causality—determining what causes something to happen. Often, doctors or other experts don't have time to thoroughly research your problem. This means *you* are the best person to conduct trial-and-error testing to find the reason.

Suppose you suspect that you have a digestive reaction to mangoes, bananas or peanuts, but you're not sure which. To find out, you test one variable (one of these foods) at a time. First, you eat mangoes, making sure you don't eat bananas or peanuts around the same time. If you experience no reaction to the mangoes, you test the same way for bananas and then peanuts. If you still have the digestive reaction after putting all three foods on trial, it's back to the drawing board.

It took me more than twenty years—and more supposed cures and more doctors than I'd care to remember—to learn that my mild headaches, lack of energy and difficulty sleeping were caused by refined sugar. I discovered this when a friend suspected that refined sugar might be the culprit. I stopped eating refined sugar for three weeks and behold—all my symptoms disappeared. I still eat fresh fruit, which contains fructose and use a sugar substitute. Trial and error and an astute friend combined to solve my problem.

73

Oh, My Aching Back!

If you haven't yet experienced back pain, here's advice that could save you from ever having it. If you already have back problems, the information may prevent your condition from worsening.

When in my twenties and thirties, I did lots of heavy lifting, both in my work and while landscaping my property. I believed, mistakenly, "if it doesn't hurt, I'm not doing anything wrong." Well, I learned recently (and you don't find this frequently published) that there's not always a sudden flash of pain to signal that you're lifting something too heavy. To the contrary, the damage is occurring as your vertebral disks are compressed without your knowing it. By the time you actually feel the pain in your back, it might be years afterward when it's often too late. The damage has been done, the disks worn out and left bulging or herniated.

The best advice is to err on the side of extreme caution. When you bring home a sack of groceries loaded with heavy cans and bottles, remove a few items and make *two* trips from car to kitchen. If you already suffer back problems, never pick up or carry anything weighing more than three or four pounds.

As mentioned in another chapter, when my wife and I travel, we carry a supply of dollar bills for tipping. We always manage to find someone to help with luggage. Everyone understands when I explain that I have back problems and would be "very grateful" for assistance. And I'm happy to be able to hand out as many $1 bills as needed. Spending an extra $50.00 on tips during a vacation keeps me pain free and out of the hospital. What a bargain!

74

Crowns and Caps

Dentists often don't tell you this: If you have gold or porcelain crowns or caps, there is always a tiny space between the edges of the crown and your gum line called the "margin." It's there because for various reasons modern dentistry cannot yet provide a perfect crown or cap that fits directly against the gum line so tightly that food or liquids cannot enter.

That gap or margin sometimes allows tiny food particles and bacteria to enter, setting up the possibility of decay. Also, the remaining stub of natural tooth under the crown is particularly susceptible to decay because it no longer is protected by its original coating of enamel. Many dentists and hygienists suggest that you can keep the tooth underneath the cap or crown clean by brushing regularly and flushing out the spaces using a Water-Pik or ViaJet (brand names) irrigation appliance. The water stream gets into spaces where a brush can't.

75

Waiting for Those Golden Years

Some folks I encounter express their intention to buy an RV, travel, or build a summer cabin when they retire. But, for many, the golden years never arrive. Sometimes a spouse takes ill or dies or a relative requires continuing care.

An actuary (the mathematics expert who is paid to predict life expectancy and such things for big insurance companies) will tell you that the chances of both you and your spouse being in good physical and financial health at retirement age are about the same as winning a lottery. Add to that the chances that you'll have responsibility for the care of older, or sometimes younger, family members.

What to do? Don't wait for the golden years to live your dreams. Do *now* what you intend to do in 20 or 30 years. You don't need to spend large amounts of money to enjoy living some of those dreams. Don't put off all your goals until after retirement.

76

Best-Kept Secret

I only wish I could recover the time, money and suffering I've spent in dental offices. Had I known as a young man what I know now, I might have been spared the pain and costs associated with having bad teeth. As far back as I can remember, my parents scheduled me for one visit a year with the dental hygienist, followed by a checkup by the dentist. Invariably, I would end up with a half-dozen cavities, and in later years some teeth required crowns, root canals or, in the worst case, extraction.

In an effort to control the damage, as an adult, I began scheduling two hygiene sessions a year. Still, I found it wasn't enough to stem the tide of dental decay. Then, about ten years ago, I started making quarterly hygiene appointments.

With quarterly cleanings and good advice from the hygienist for at-home dental hygiene, I finally managed to break the cycle. Since then, I've had no more than two or three teeth requiring a dentist's attention, and of those, two were bad wisdom teeth that required removal.

The sad fact is that no one in any dental office anywhere encouraged me to have more frequent cleanings. I've found that what I pay the hygienist for frequent cleanings and solid advice is considerably less than the cost of restorative dental work, gold crowns and root canals. Not to mention the pain and/or discomfort.

77

How to Reduce Your Stress

Only recently has modern medicine accepted the premise that stress often can be the cause of disorders such as high blood pressure, ulcers, heart attack and even cancer. But, what are the solutions for reducing anxiety?

Over the years, people have tried releasing their frustration on the tennis court, jogging path or hiking trails; through hypnotism, doctor's prescriptions and biofeedback; or by resorting to alcohol or illegal drugs. As a graduate student, I was once assigned to review all research data available on stress reduction. While searching through the archives, I came across an article published in a professional journal in the 1930s by a noted researcher. To my astonishment, he concluded that after almost a lifetime of inquiry into the subject, he was convinced that the only truly effective means of reducing anxiety was to *remove* the anxiety-creating stimulus. Nothing less. A stockbroker neighbor puts it this way: "You have to sell (stocks that are worrying you) until you can sleep."

If this notion appears simplistic, think about it. You might have an investment or there might be a person who is making your life unbearable. But does there exist much likelihood that a boss or a mother-in-law would suddenly realize how stressful their conduct makes you feel and suddenly change their ways? Rather than trying to cope with an unpleasant situation, consider applying the researcher's findings: Tell your boss or your mother-in-law how you feel. Say that you need their help in resolving the situation that makes you uncomfortable. If they are amenable to working out a mutually agreeable solution, you have removed the anxiety-creating stimulus. If they won't oblige, tell them that you see two doors, one leading to cooperation, the other to your departure. Should they continue to reject your attempts, you must be prepared to pay the price—the loss of your job or marriage. The price of doing nothing might be costlier.

I am often reminded of the words of Jacque Fresco, to whom this book is dedicated. He said: "The secret to life is knowing when to hang in there and when to get off."

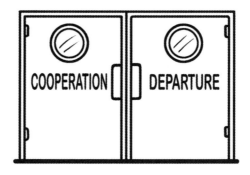

78

Walk!

If you are active in sports, you probably get enough exercise. But, if you don't get regular exercise or can't do strenuous activity, walking might be your answer. I try to walk for an hour, five days a week. I choose routes where I don't encounter much vehicular traffic and where I can enjoy the landscape.

In summer, I walk in the early morning when it's cool and in winter I schedule walks for later when it's a bit warmer. I take along a Walkman to listen to music or National Public Radio. Sometimes, I switch and listen to an audio cassette of a book or a seminar. Thus, I don't feel bored or that I'm wasting an hour's time. I won't dwell on the importance of exercise because it seems that every other day there's a new report in the media citing results of studies that support the benefits of walking.

79

Oxymoron: A Healthy Tan

The title of this chapter is an oxymoron because there is no such thing as a tan that's healthy.

Despite frequent warnings from health experts, sunbathers continue to expose their bodies to harmful ultraviolet rays. I see these sun worshippers lying poolside for hours on end, seeking the golden tan that they believe will make them appear healthy and beautiful. What they may not know is that ultraviolet rays *accumulate* in the body, not showing their effects until a person is 40 or 50 years old. By then, it's too late. The least possible damage is prematurely wrinkled skin. Some people will end up with skin cancer or, perhaps, worse, melanoma, which can be fatal.

I knew a young woman in California whose work required her to spend many hours outdoors. Instead of protecting her skin, she wore shorts, a tank top, sandals and no hat. By the time she was 35, she had the leathery complexion of a 70-year-old ranch hand. Fair-skinned people or redheads are at even greater risk.

As a youngster growing up in South Florida, I spent hours on the beaches clad only in swim trunks. It was when I reached my twenties, moved to California and joined a hiking club that I learned about the dangers of prolonged exposure to the sun. Since then, I have not ventured outdoors without wearing long sleeves and a wide-brimmed hat. I also use a sunscreen with a high rating.

86

Health Newsletters

Keeping up with the latest developments in health and wellness can help you avoid serious medical problems. There is a myriad of health-focused consumer newsletters containing facts about the newest treatments, results of important studies and tips for improving health. I began subscribing to several of these publications years ago and I can directly attribute numerous health benefits to what I've gleaned from them. One newsletter focuses exclusively on warnings about dangerous pills and supplements.

I also subscribe to nutrition newsletters so I'll know what I'm putting into my body. While the processors of fast foods and junk foods don't often warn me about such things as trans-fatty acids and saturated fat, I can count on these newsletters to keep me informed. They cover a surprisingly wide range, from packaged foods to fast-food restaurants' menu items.

Whenever I can treat a problem using natural methods, such as a change of diet or exercise program, I feel I'm better off. I also use the Internet to search for the most risk-free or least invasive approaches to maintaining or improving my health. However, I always caution that before making any decision related to your health, you should consult your physician.

81

Commuting's Hidden Costs

Before it became an accepted fact that exposure to traffic stress can result in serious illness, I already rejected long, rush-hour commutes. I either adjusted my schedule to avoid driving during rush hours, or when that wasn't possible, I moved closer to my work. When I lived in the San Francisco Bay area, I knew people who commuted more than two hours daily on crowded, congested freeways. Often, before reaching the age of forty, their nerves were wrecked and they were frequently ill. One man I knew, who later died of leukemia, told me he felt that his years of commuting were responsible for his loss of health.

My own feelings on this subject are that commuting on clogged highways is a form of unconsciously injuring yourself. If you submit to this type of redundant stress on a daily basis, ask yourself why.

There are other options. Rail transportation is one of the best alternatives because you can read, work or sleep en route. Try flexible work hours or telecommute from your home or move nearer to your work. I once turned down an offer of a good-paying job because I could find no alternative to a harrowing daily commute of more than an hour each way. If you come away with the impression that I'm strident on this issue, you're right. Long commutes aren't good for you, your family, your car, or the environment.

82

Four-Legged Stress Relievers

A few years ago, when my aunt's dog came to live with us, I was wary. My aunt had died and the dog needed a home. She was a seven-year-old Boston terrier and completely housebroken. A friend encouraged me, saying that dogs are wonderful stress-relievers. I smiled, but didn't really believe it.

I do believe it now. We have had Teddie for more than five years and she has been a joy. Often, after getting off the phone with a difficult caller, I find myself petting Teddie or sometimes even talking to her. She is always understanding and caring. I frankly don't know how I lived so many years without a dog in my life.

83

Fax the Doctor

Have you ever tried to ask your doctor a question via phone? If so, lots of luck. Doctors are busy, busy, busy. Often, you are asked to leave your question with a receptionist. Or perhaps leave a voicemail message for the doctor's assistant. Sometimes calls are returned.

Recently, my wife came up with an alternative for reaching the doctor. She was helping a friend contact her physician and, as expected, encountered the above-mentioned obstacles.

So, she decided to use the fax software which came bundled in our computer and sent a fax message to the doctor. She first phoned the doctor's office and asked the receptionist for their fax number. Then she and her friend composed a brief letter to the doctor stating the patient's need.

Within an hour, she received a call from the doctor's assistant asking her to come in that same day. Normally, her doctor books appointments weeks ahead.

Since then, when phoned messages prove ineffective, we use our fax to contact medical offices.

Business

84

Compromise Is King

When negotiating, the other person will always respond more favorably if it appears that you are willing to meet him halfway. This is another way of saying "split the difference."

Yes, you'll have to give a little, as will the other person, but you'll more likely swing your deal.

If you decide to give nothing, there's a good chance that's what you'll end up with—nothing.

85

Never Cry 'Wolf!'

A lesson I learned as a child from a fairytale book has served me well: Never cry "Wolf!" Over the years I was in business, I developed trusting one-on-one relationships with various vendors and tradespeople. I made it a point never to disturb them after hours or on weekends. However, on those rare occasions when I had a real emergency, they never failed to come through.

I know others who don't adhere to this policy and cry "Wolf!" virtually every week it seems. Soon, they find that when they're in a real pinch, nobody heeds their call.

In a similar vein, I seldom call on people for favors. If someone owes me a favor, I save it for when I'm truly in need.

86

Pay 'Em to Go Away

When a sub-par performance by a service provider leaves you fuming, it may be best to cut your ties with that person. Of course, your first response should be to ask for the problem or mistake to be corrected. But if a second effort doesn't satisfy you, forget it. It's not going to get better.

Don't be vindictive. Just pay the person what's been agreed upon and walk away. You'll be getting off more cheaply and with less frustration than if you stick it out to the bitter end.

I learned this lesson the hard way when, a few years ago, I hired a licensed electrician to fix a minor problem. The man returned six times and then he and his boss together made eight more visits without finding a solution. Eventually, they stopped returning my calls.

Then, I contacted a handyman, who fixed the problem immediately and permanently. I learned from this experience that if a service provider doesn't have the skill to solve a problem, additional requests aren't going to make him any more knowledgeable.

87

A 'Can-Do' Attitude

The bigger the company or business, the more likely you'll hear, "No way we can do that." Compare this to the owner of a mom-and-pop business who's more likely to respond, "We've never done that before, but I'm sure we can find a way." A "can-do" attitude is valuable whether you're the customer or the vendor.

Buyers of goods and services are not naive. They know the value of personal service. This includes purchasing agents and those in charge of outsourcing at major corporations. If they have a choice between obtaining a service from another large corporation or from a self-employed individual—especially if it's a rush job that's needed "yesterday"—they'll often choose the latter. Why? Because they know that if they call the big corporation, they'll be provided with a dozen reasons why their request is impossible to fill. The small owner/operator, however, is more likely to be willing to work over the weekend if necessary to make sure your job gets done.

If you're an employee, the "can-do" attitude will serve you well, too. When the boss announces at 3 p.m. that someone needs to work late to ensure that an order is ready for an important customer the next morning, you be the one to respond, "I'll take care of it. It'll be ready in the morning." What do you think *that* will do for your career?

88

Listen to Experience

Not long ago, I wrote a "thank-you" letter to a man who saved me from wasting a year of my life and several thousand dollars. What did he do? He cautioned me *not* to enter into a business venture I was considering.

As I wrote to him, I was struck by the thought that seldom are people who save others from dire consequences ever properly acknowledged.

In my case, the man was a family friend with many years of experience in the publishing business, including that of printing and distributing postcards. I had conceived the idea of working with a photographer friend to print and distribute glossy postcards with photos of the natural wonders of Southern Arizona.

I outlined my business plan and mailed it to the family friend, who was then retired. He replied with a thoughtful letter, sharing his insights and detailing the many obstacles and risks inherent in the business along with the unpredictability of market conditions.

I'll always remember his bottom line: "George, this business is not for you." After reading his letter, I showed it to my wife and my photographer friend. We had absolutely no hesitation in scrapping the idea and considered ourselves fortunate to have had access to an expert's advice.

89

Connections Count

When you hire an expert, sometimes the expert's connections are even more important than her own qualifications.

Not long ago, a friend settled a long-standing dispute with the Internal Revenue Service. For almost ten years, this individual had written letters, hired high-priced lawyers and tried virtually everything to resolve the matter, only to discover that all doors were barred to reaching anyone in the IRS who had decision-making authority.

Then, one day my friend was referred to a retired IRS agent who specialized in handling such matters and knew exactly how to open doors. Within a few months, the case was resolved.

It is no secret that certain lawyers and law firms get better results appearing before certain judges than do others. The same applies to getting access to officials in government or other public agencies. If you hire the "right" architectural firm or builder or law firm to represent you in seeking a variance or building permit, your chances of approval are greatly increased. In contrast, there are people who will hire a zealot or other controversial figure to represent them. The zealot will produce fireworks at the hearing, but in the end, the application is denied. Remember, often it's not what you know, but who you know.

90

The 'Big Deal'

As a producer and publisher of newsletters, I'd often get excited over the prospect of a possible "big deal" order. I'd rush around putting together massive proposals, taking pains to ensure that everything I submitted was just perfect. Bottom line every time: zilch.

By contrast, a prospect would phone to inquire about a small or modest-sized order or contract, a short meeting would follow and I'd get the business.

My guess is that many of those who phone out of the blue for a price quote on a large-figure contract already know who is going to get it. More often than not your caller needs to furnish his boss with three bids because that's company policy.

After chasing a couple dozen of these "big deals," I wised up and began quoting a price on the phone or sending an e-mail of a few lines. If the prospective customer wanted a detailed proposal, I'd reply that I'd have to bill him for that service because it required several hours of my time. That usually ended the conversation. Summing it up: Don't invest much of your time in "big deals." They seldom pan out.

91

Play the Odds

Let's say you're looking for a job. One choice is to apply where you know there will be several hundred or perhaps more than 1,000 applicants. It's a super position, but your chance of success might be better in a lottery. You also learn of another opening that is not quite as high-paying or prestigious, but one that will attract only a half-dozen applicants. If you are confident of your qualifications, where do you focus your time and energies?

Don't waste time pursuing opportunities where the chances of success are slim at best. How many athletes play in the major leagues? How many stars are there in Hollywood? When your chances are 10,000-to-1 or 100,000-to-1, why not reconsider your plans?

Perhaps the most valuable college course I took was statistics. It was one of those required courses, and at first I wasn't eager to enroll. But what I learned about bell curves and probabilities has served me well to this day. I also absorbed some extra knowledge about the mathematics of chance by having attended thoroughbred races with my grandfather. However, it's important to know that the laws of probability extend well beyond the racetrack and the job-seeking arena.

Several years ago, before I launched a business-oriented subscription newsletter, we did a test mailing to 2,000 prospects drawn from a potential mailing list of 10,000 company names. Approximately two percent of those receiving the promotional mailing responded by returning a subscription ordercard. Normally, a one percent return is considered good. We launched the newsletter and subsequently mailed promotional packets to all 10,000 names on the list, receiving the same two percent return.

Using probability percentages also extends to making important medical decisions. What are the risks involved? In the past, such figures, especially those involving surgery, were not readily available, and doctors were not always eager to provide them to their patients. Now, much of this information can be obtained through an Internet search. Once you have these figures in hand, you are in a better position to make your decision.

Risk management is an important skill which can help you get through life.

92

How Is My Case Coming Along?

One of the most memorable movie scenes I recall came from an adaptation of Kafka's *The Trial*. I use this inspiration whenever I have to deal with bureaucracy or red tape either in business or government.

In the movie, a tired, middle-aged man enters a cavernous structure filled with hundreds of long tables. He makes his way through the labyrinth to where a white-bearded attorney in a rumpled dark suit sits behind one of the tables.

The audience is subtly informed that the man has been paying this same visit every day for the last 18 years. We hear the man ask, "How is my case coming along?" The lawyer speaks not one word of dialog. He only nods. The visitor then takes his briefcase and departs.

Whenever I think I'm getting the runaround in corporate or government offices—whether it's about an application, a pending refund or an order I placed—I pose the tired man's question to the paper-shufflers who answer the phone. "How's my case coming along?" I ask. I always request to speak to the same person (that's very important!) and I'm always extra polite, if not apologetic. However, I remain persistent to the extreme.

If you phone every day or two, but remain friendly and polite, your respondent will have no legitimate reason to complain to her supervisor about your persistence. She will decide sooner or later that it's easier to do what has to be done to satisfy you than to keep answering your phone calls. Not once since I began doing this fifteen years ago has anyone yet asked me, "Case? What case?"

93

Collecting Receivables

Bad debts don't have to be part of doing business. I produced newsletters for Silicon Valley companies for more than 16 years during which time I was never stuck for one penny of bad debt—although I encountered a couple of close calls.

I followed the advice I was given many years earlier as a newspaper delivery boy. It was: Never let anyone get into you for more than you can comfortably afford to lose. The advice was sage. Unfortunately, I received it after several subscribers moved away without paying their newspaper bills amounting to a couple of months' charges. I ended up eating the charges, but as a result I learned a valuable lesson.

Having learned that lesson and taken it into business with me, when I performed work for a new customer, I always politely explained that I was a small businessman and needed to work on a system of "progress payments." That meant one-third due on approval of the draft copy, one-third on approval of final proofs and the balance within 30 days of delivery.

If the payments weren't forthcoming, I was in a position to pull the plug at any time and end up with a relatively minor loss. And, of course, I never started work on a company's new issue until the previous one was fully paid.

There was an exception, however. When producing a newsletter for a blue chip company, I billed in full when the job was completed—no "progress payments."

One of my close calls involved a company rumored to be close to filing bankruptcy. My contact within the company told me that suing to collect would be a waste of my money. So, instead I used a version of the "How Is My Case Coming Along?" routine (see previous chapter).

I phoned virtually anyone in the company who would take my calls, each time being polite, but at the same time offering a big sob story about how we were being pressed by our own creditors.

I wanted them to empathize with me, rather than view me as just another creditor.

After several weeks, I learned from my contact that the company's finance office had received payment on a substantial account, and for a brief period had funds to pay some of its outstanding bills—one of them mine.

Just a few weeks later, the company did file for bankruptcy. Whew! Close call.

94

Defensive Entrepreneurship

Today almost no job is secure. Recent statistics show that the average length of employment is from 18 to 24 months. That might be okay if you're 22 years old and just out of college—or maybe pushing 30.

But, if you are nearing 40 or are older and have a number of years invested in a company, it can be a major concern to know that you can be downsized or terminated (sometimes as a result of age discrimination) at any time. Few employers want to hire people in their forties or fifties, especially those who are already near the top of the pay scale.

The Wall Street Journal featured a story about some workers who positioned themselves "ahead of the curve" in this context. The *Journal* called them "defensive entrepreneurs" because each had prepared for the possibility of layoff or downsizing by establishing a part-time business operated from home.

Their common goal: to expand their businesses to the point where the business could someday support them. Meanwhile, should the ax fall, these part-time entrepreneurs would have a job and an income, albeit a modest income, while they either seek another position or grow their part-time businesses into full-time operations.

95

When the Customer Is A Walking Headache

After being employed for many years and working with a super bunch of people, there came a day when things at the job changed. New management took over. Until then, I had looked forward to going to work and I never found myself watching the clock. Since I wasn't in a position to choose my bosses, I decided to leave and go into business for myself. From the outset, I was determined to work only with nice people—and people I could trust.

But, because I was hungry that first year, I reluctantly took on a customer whom I sensed would be a headache. And was he ever! I had quoted the customer a flat rate for my services, but his extra demands, change orders and reversed decisions cost me dearly. After finally completing the work, I notified the customer that I would no longer be available to serve him.

That experience taught me that not only is it stressful and unpleasant to work with people who don't treat you considerately, but that maintaining a business relationship with them is also unprofitable.

Now, years later, I can spot one of these "walking headaches" the moment they come through the door. However, to remain courteous, I make myself go through the motions of listening to their needs, after which I tell them that I'll check to see if I have someone available who can perform the requested service. The next day, I inform them via phone that no one appropriate is available for their assignment.

I haven't regretted maintaining my "nice-folks-only" policy. Although I never became a tycoon, I can say that I have had wonderful business relationships with both customers and vendors, some lasting more than fifteen years.

96

Avoiding 'No Shows'

Whether it's for a personal or professional meeting, people often fail to keep appointments.

Not long ago, after driving more than twenty miles to meet with a prospective client—and being stood up—I decided it was time to take a tip from my dentist. Now, I telephone the day before any appointment to confirm it.

If I reach the person's voice mail, I request a return call. If I don't get a call back, I phone again early the next morning, leaving word that I'm waiting for his call before proceeding. Under no circumstances do I leave home until I'm certain that I have a confirmed appointment.

This policy applies to social appointments as well as business meetings. Time is too precious to waste a couple of hours—or in some instances a half-day (if you live in an area of heavy traffic and long commutes)—simply because an inconsiderate individual either has a bad memory or doesn't value me or my time.

97

Stay Ahead of the Curve

Some years ago, I wrote a newsletter article about a hotel executive noted for his ability to "see beyond tomorrow."

Fellow hoteliers remarked that he always accurately sensed when to jump aboard a new trend. When he spotted a move toward all-suite hotels, for example, he weighed the cost of renovation and construction against the cost of being left out. He consulted his staff and outside advisers, considered all the facts, then made his decision.

Is this executive unique? Certainly not. Many individuals—not only the big movers and shakers—can easily stand as his equal. Most important is that you keep abreast of news and developments, particularly in areas which affect your bottom line.

And it's not always knowing when to jump aboard. Sometimes, keeping ahead of the curve means knowing when to jump off.

My much-quoted and admired relative, Uncle Max, ended all of our telephone conversations with these words: "Remember, my boy, you must always keep one step ahead of the crowd. One step ahead!" He was right.

98

Don't Pay Overhead

I've operated part-time and full-time businesses from home for more than thirty years, and have never paid for a business telephone line. I've never paid rent for an office.

I subcontract all work that I don't perform myself, and so that means I don't have any employees. I pay no unemployment insurance, no workers compensation, no payroll tax. In short, I operate on a shoestring.

But, as frugal as I am, when it comes to the quality of my work, I spare no effort.

I've watched other entrepreneurs start up new businesses. Immediately, they rent and furnish an office, hire a secretary and employees and eat lunches at trendy restaurants. These expenses are among the reasons why so many new business ventures fail.

A few years ago, a client for whom I produced a company newsletter at a rock-bottom price asked me when I was going to get an office. I responded, "When you're ready to pay for it."

He smiled and never said anything further about my getting an office.

If your ego can stand it, skip showing off. Drive an older car and avoid taking on any debt. Keeping your business solvent is more important than anything else.

99

The Bank of George

Many small-business persons share a common problem—how to obtain a loan to expand their business or meet short-term cash needs. Most banks aren't interested in loaning money to small businesses, especially home-based businesses. As a result, many people in this predicament go from lender to lender, frustrated by waiting and red tape and, in the end, not getting their loan. They then do the worst thing possible—borrow cash on credit cards that carry interest rates of up to 21 percent.

I solved this problem by becoming my own banker when The Bank of George was founded. During one year, instead of buying a new car or going on a vacation, I lived austerely and saved every penny until I accumulated a nest egg of $5,000. I put that money into my business account with a red-lined "Hands Off!" The money was to be used *only* for paying creditors while awaiting payment from my customers. As soon as the customer paid, the principal was returned to this special temporary loan account. It was *never* used for any other purpose.

The amount of interest I paid for business loans during the eighteen years I was producing newsletters? Zero. The worry and frustration I experienced in connection with business loans? Zero. A side benefit is that my vendors loved to do business with me because I always paid their bills the *same day* that I received them. My temporary loan fund enabled me to do this. It was no surprise that my vendors never hesitated when I asked for a special favor. And they always kept their prices low.

100

The Soft Sell

Many people who sell goods or services fail to catch the subtleties that separate "yes" from "no" or "I'd like to think about it."

Supervisors always urge a salesperson to follow up on calls, and sales experts tend to advocate this approach, too. But in all the years I was employed, and later as an independent businessman, I cannot recall a single instance in which a follow-up call produced positive results.

I'd dutifully make the follow-up call and sometimes be told icily, "Mr. Newman, I have your card and I'll call you when I'm ready." Besides irritating the potential customer, I'd wasted my time.

Now, my approach is to give it my best shot during the initial presentation. I offer my product or service at the most competitive price, then leave the decision to the prospect. I've sometimes received callbacks as long as a year after making a presentation.

Don't badger a customer by repeating the sales pitch if they don't have any interest. Your time is valuable. Go on to the next lead.

101

The Deadline Before The Deadline

Everyone knows what it is to race against a deadline. When white-knuckle time arrives, we rush to the fax machine or Federal Express.

But you can meet deadlines without the stress. Build a time cushion into any project that has a firm deadline date. Always allow for the possibility that something is going to pop up in your life or someone you're counting on will cause a delay. With a cushion, you can suffer the delay and still make your deadline.

If you're facing a deadline—even if you have plenty of time—don't tell a tradesman or repair person that you're not in hurry. When I'm working with a subcontractor, I never reveal my customer's actual deadline. If the work needs to be completed no later than May 1, I tell him that my customer needs the work completed no later than April 27. Using this cushion, I've never missed a deadline.

When my wife and I travel, I always set my deadline for having all packing and other arrangements completed at least one day before our actual departure. And guess what? There's never any spare time left. Something always comes up at the last minute. That's when a time cushion saves us again.

102

To Be or Not to Be Self-Employed?

We live in uncertain times. For that reason self-employment may be a better choice now than it was in our parents' or grandparents' generation.

However, it's not for everyone. Striking out on your own requires a certain type of personality, which can't be learned. If the prospect of owning your own business or being self-employed causes you to lose sleep, don't let anyone push you into it.

Let's start with the drawbacks of self-employment. Though you won't have to punch a time clock, you will find yourself working nights, weekends and even holidays if that's what it takes to succeed. You'll have no health care coverage other than what you supply for yourself. Neither will you be guaranteed periodic raises or paid vacations. No one will hand you a paycheck, and you can count on having to juggle your finances so that only the most important bills get paid while the others are stacked in priority order.

Now, for the advantages. No one can fire you. There usually will be *some* money coming in, though seldom as much as you would like. Best of all, perhaps, is that no one can decide when it's time for you to be downsized, laid off or retire. I've seen employees dumped on the junk heap while still in their forties. Some never recovered; others became embittered or ill. If you're self-employed, you can work as long as your health allows, scale back to part-time or sell your business and retire.

When I lived in California and operated my own small business, I attended weekly breakfasts at a downtown cafe where a dozen or more entrepreneurs met regularly. It was an opportunity for independents, such as myself, to network with others.

I'll always remember one morning when a middle-aged man, who was experiencing a period of financial downturn, was asked whether he might consider giving up his business and seek employment.

"Things are tough right now," he replied. "But, there's no way I could ever go back to working for someone else."

I looked around the long table and saw all the others nod in agreement. They understood. They'd crossed a line when they started working for themselves and none were going back.

103

Repetitive Tasks

If you are industrious or creative—or both—you shouldn't waste time on repetitive tasks even if the work is for your own business.

I have a friend who thinks nothing of spending eight to ten hours folding flyers or stuffing envelopes for a promotional mailing.

He boasts that he can do the work while watching television, thereby saving money. But is he *really* saving money?

He's unswayed when I point out that he can hire a mailing house or letter shop which uses machines to fold and stuff at a cost of about a penny apiece. That's why such machines were invented, I tell him.

My friend spends his time, which could be used more productively, to save trivial amounts.

Before you take on a repetitive task, ask yourself what the cost in time is to you and whether your time couldn't be better spent.

104

When a 'Stop-Loss' Is Needed

Almost as important as knowing when to hang in there is observing the maxim, "Don't throw good money after bad."

I learned this from a friend when as a young man I was about to sink several hundred dollars more into a used car which had undergone endless repairs and was financially devouring me. After considering the advice, I decided to scrap the car.

The same advice applies to business, real estate and other investments. Good business people recognize when they've made a mistake or if a condition changes, and they take steps to cut their losses. Others will stick to their guns, no matter the cost, rather than write off a bad investment or admit to making a mistake.

105

The Results of Doing Nothing

On a Sunday afternoon several years ago, a group of newsletter publishers met in the garden of a San Francisco Bay Area couple to swap experiences on effective marketing ideas.

One of the participants, a folksy gentleman, said something, although seemingly simplistic, that has remained with me to this day. "The bottom line," he declared, "is that when you don't do anything, nothing happens."

In the ensuing months, I noticed that when I didn't make an active effort to market my newsletter, there was a sharp dropoff in orders. Then I'd remember the savvy advice and get busy

$$0 + 0 = 0$$

106

Being Stingy Is a Mistake

Recently, my wife and I joined another couple for lunch at a neighborhood restaurant. Everyone ordered a full meal, and when the entrees were served the husband asked the waiter for some extra grated cheese for his pasta dish. The waiter returned with the requested grated cheese, but when the bill arrived the husband was irate. There had been a charge of 75 cents added for a tiny paper cup of grated cheese.

The husband complained to the owner (it was an independently-owned restaurant) and was informed that there is always a charge for extra grated cheese. Needless to say, the couple vowed never to return to that restaurant again.

Certainly, if the husband had made an extravagant request, he might have accepted the extra charge. But, since he had ordered a pasta dish and the grated cheese provided was insufficient, it seemed that he was not asking for the moon.

In adding the extra charge, the owner alienated everyone at our table. Didn't he realize that he was turning away perhaps several hundreds of dollars of business per year? Not to mention the bad publicity that would be generated every time the husband told his story to yet another acquaintance.

Small-minded thinking never gets anyone anywhere. Be generous whenever you can. My experience has been that acts of generosity always come back to you. Many times over.

107

Benefit from Your Own Ideas

If you're an innovative person and are employed in a confining work environment, you might need to make a change, perhaps, even work for yourself.

I once worked for a company where I presented management with new product ideas and suggestions for cost efficiency at least a half-dozen times over a period of years. These were among ideas that I had earlier bounced off my colleagues, many of which I discarded when I realized that they weren't workable. I submitted only those that had stood the test of peer criticism and evaluation. The bottom line is that management accepted none of my ideas. They made me feel that even the time they took to consider my suggestions was a gesture of tolerance. The clear message was to "Just do your job and don't bother us with your ideas."

I got the message loud and clear and said to myself, "You folks don't need me or my ideas."

Once I had my finances in good shape, I left the company and went into business for myself. I came up with more new ideas and asked for feedback from my self-employed friends. Some of my ideas were put into action, with some failing and others succeeding. I never struck it rich, but always made a living. Most important, however, was that I no longer felt frustrated. Of course, there were risks, but the responsibility for deciding when to take them was mine.

108

When Expedience Pays

There are times when one should stick to his principles and there are other occasions when expedience makes more sense.

A fine example is a situation that occurred a few years ago when I was trying to sell a vacant single-family house. It was located in a solid middle-class neighborhood surrounded by mostly well-maintained houses. The exception was the property next door to the house I owned. The front yard looked like a jungle and was turning off prospective buyers.

I considered calling on the homeowner and asking him to clean up the yard, but decided such a move would most likely be counterproductive. Instead, when the landscape maintenance crew I had hired arrived to service my property, I took aside the crew's boss and whispered in his ear.

A few minutes later, he walked up to the house next door, rang the bell, and told the homeowner that he was working in the neighborhood that day and needed some extra work to keep his crew busy. He offered to trim and clean up their entire front yard for only $10.00. His offer was quickly accepted.

An hour later the former eyesore front yard looked magnificent. Yes, of course, I had paid the crew's boss an extra $75.00 cash to do the work, but a week later my property sold.

Time Savers

109

Skip the Commercials

Approximately fifteen minutes of every television hour—often more—are devoted to commercials (public broadcasting channels excepted). If you watch the tube four hours a day, you're exposed to an hour of commercials. Carry that further and it comes out to seven hours a week, 30 hours a month, or 364 hours a year of commercials.

My wife and I have opted to do more productive things with our time than allow ourselves to be consumed by commercials. First, we don't view much commercial television. Instead, we prefer PBS, C-SPAN or CNN and a few selected programs on other networks. We record many of these programs to watch later while eating dinner. However, that doesn't mean we'll just let the recorded program run uninterrupted. No way. With remote control in hand, we fast-forward through any commercials.

And if there's a segment in the program that doesn't interest us, we fast forward through that, too. In the end, we've viewed only the portions that we want to watch—commercial-free. This allows us time after dinner to pursue other interests. Since there are a limited number of discretionary hours available to us, it's important to use them wisely.

110

Hands-Free Phones

Can you recall a day when you haven't been put on hold at least once?

One of the best investments I ever made was when I bought my first telephone headset. Today, I wouldn't be without one. A headset frees both hands so that I can write, leaf through catalogs or use the computer while on hold.

Using a headset also is more comfortable than holding the handset to your ear for long periods.

I never place a call from home unless I'm at my desk where I have my headset. If I'm put on hold, I can work on the computer, pay some bills, or simply read. I would estimate that the headset enables me to make productive use of not less than a half-hour a week of otherwise dead time.

111

Curb Those Telemarketers

Hardly anything is more annoying than being interrupted by a telephone solicitor during dinner or while watching your favorite TV program. My wife and I used to receive two or three telemarketer calls every evening. At the time, we didn't have an effective response except to say we weren't interested. That only brought out the telemarketer's "overcoming obstacles" script.

We now have a multifaceted plan to deal with this problem and it's been reinforced by passage of the federal DO NOT CALL statute which imposes heavy penalties on companies which disregard an individual's request for privacy. However, some categories are exempted from the law. So, it's not a slam dunk yet. Be sure to register your name and phone number with the government's DO NOT CALL database if you don't want these calls.

Our telephone answering machine is connected to our primary residence phone to screen calls when we don't want to be disturbed. Rarely will a phone solicitor leave a message. We monitor our incoming calls and if after the beep we hear a voice, we usually answer. If we don't want to hear the telephone ring at all, such as when we're taking a nap, we temporarily switch off the phone bell, set the volume on the answering machine to zero and let the answering machine silently take calls.

If we inadvertently answer a call from a telemarketer, we say: "I'm sorry, but we are not permitted to accept phone solicitations at this number. Would you kindly remove this name and number from your list." Most solicitors will comply, especially since passage of the DO NOT CALL legislation.

Many local telephone companies publish directories with a heavy black dot or star adjacent to the name of subscribers who do not wish to receive phone solicitations. You can opt for this service for a small monthly fee. You also can send your name, address and phone number to direct marketing associations and request to be removed from their lists.

Another option is to switch to an unlisted number, although some people must maintain a published number for customers or clients. If you do request to be unlisted, don't ask for a new phone number. You never know whose former phone number you're getting. Often, you're better off keeping your own.

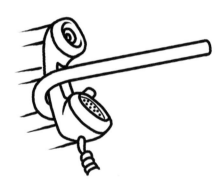

112

Avoid Congestion, Delays

A busy person is usually productive, but that person can accomplish even more by scheduling activities in off-peak hours. My wife and I schedule our outside activities, whether it's grocery shopping or running errands, when other people aren't doing the same thing. The hours wasted in traffic or standing in line can *never* be recovered.

Even at home, you can benefit from making business phone calls during off-peak hours. At government agencies and private sector businesses that handle a high volume of consumer calls, it's a cinch that at 9 a.m. on Monday you'll spend some time on hold. Find out when the least busiest time is at these places and call then.

If you want to beat the heavy traffic, it's best to go out after 9 a.m. when most adults are working. Return home before 2 p.m. when the afternoon traffic starts to build. If you're working 9 to 5, there are some things you can do to save time. One of these is running errands during your lunch break. That's what I did when I worked normal hours. Later, when I was self-employed, I always scheduled business appointments at mid-morning.

If a customer or prospective customer proposed meeting during the afternoon, I always offered a reason or excuse for requesting a morning appointment. Otherwise, I knew that I would spend at least 90 minutes stuck in heavy traffic getting there and the same amount of time or more returning home. I couldn't afford to spend three hours behind the wheel of my car. This technique worked for many years, and I never lost a customer as a result.

Another tip: If you regularly encounter a bottleneck during your commute, don't despair. Look for an alternative route or alter your driving schedule by a few minutes.

For instance, I've discovered that if I drive on a main thoroughfare between 7:30 and 8 a.m. the traffic is bumper to bumper. But, at exactly 8:01 a.m., there are 50 percent fewer cars on that street. The reason? Thousands of individuals must report for work at 8 a.m. The next group of commuters is due at work at 8:30 and a few more at 9.

If you enter the thoroughfare at exactly 8:01, you have a good chance of encountering less traffic for the next ten minutes or so, which is often enough time for you to get where you need to go.

Finally, if there's something you've always wanted to do, but which requires fighting your way through a crowd, consider this: Go on Super Bowl Sunday when millions of Americans are glued to their television sets at home.

The small amount of time you invest in solving traffic or other congestion problems will pay off many times over in reduced frustration.

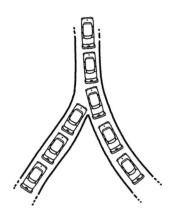

113

Voice Mail Saves Time

Imagine how much time is wasted playing telephone tag. Whether our telephone call involves a business or personal matter, we usually encounter voice mail or a home answering machine. Most callers then leave their names and numbers, saying, "Please call me back." Instead, why not just say what you would have said had you reached the person?

I often have transacted complex matters via voice mail—going back and forth with substantive messages as many as a half-dozen times—without ever speaking directly with the person I was calling.

114

The Missing Spoon Solution

Think of how often you're in a restaurant and can't attract the attention of your waiter or waitress. Maybe you need only an extra spoon or some cream for your coffee, but you wait, wait, wait.

I was one of those frustrated patrons until my wife showed me there's an alternative.

She waits a moment, but if she can't catch our server's eye, she leaves the table and walks over to either our server or the nearest server station and politely requests whatever is needed.

I was impressed—and amazed—that I had never considered doing that. Now, I do.

And guess what? I'm no longer among those who are frustrated watching their pancakes get cold while hoping that their server will eventually remember to bring the maple syrup.

115

Emergency Cash

Sometimes, I leave the house and forget to take my wallet. When I arrive at a store, post office or supermarket, I realize my mental lapse and have to return home.

No more. My wife suggested that I keep an envelope containing a $20 bill in the glove compartment of my car. I can't tell you how many times it's saved me.

116

If It Ain't Broke

Something new—whether it's a gadget or a major purchase—is nice, but it can bring new problems. At the urging of a friend, I reluctantly downloaded a free, updated version of a certain software, even when the program I had was doing *exactly* what I needed it to do.

As it turned out, it took me and a high-priced computer expert most of the following week to undo the problems created by the installation of the new program. That was the last time I made an exception to the axiom: "If it ain't broke, don't fix it."

117

Managing Time

William Ewart Gladstone, a nineteenth-century British statesman, served sixty-three of his eighty-nine years in the House of Commons. He was elected prime minister four times and pursued scholarly interests throughout his life. Although he took advantage of every breathing moment, one of his biographers, Roy Jenkins, wrote of Gladstone's "endless battle for the victory of activity over time." There was never enough time to satisfy him.

In reading this book, you will have noticed that many of the suggestions relate to time management. As a young man, this was never a major concern for me. I wish now that it had been.

I recently spoke with a man in his fifties who enjoys hiking and camping, but is frustrated because his job keeps him from spending more time in his leisure pursuit. He said to me, "Look, I'm not one of those types who spend their time on the couch watching 'I Love Lucy' reruns. I realize that the time when I can do strenuous hiking is running out."

Most of us discover this reality too late. Isn't how we use our time the true measure of what we do with our lives?

118

'It'll Just Be a Few Minutes...'

How often have you been informed when entering a restaurant or coffee shop that "It'll be just a few minutes" for a table? If you're not in a hurry, there might be no problem with that. But, if you need to get back to work or have other appointments or obligations, a "short wait" can end up being a long wait and spell disaster for your plans.

Not long ago, my wife and I were traveling through the Southwest and stopped overnight in a Texas city. The desk clerk recommended a trendy restaurant nearby. When we arrived, the large parking lot was nearly full and the waiting area filled with customers standing in line. We checked with the hostess and were informed that there would be "just a short wait."

Suspiciously eyeing the throng of waiting customers, I asked approximately how long the wait might be. "About 45 minutes," the hostess replied. I added our name to the waiting list, then promptly asked a customer standing in line how long he and his wife had been waiting. He informed me that they had been there an hour-and-a-half. My wife and I headed for the door and settled for a less popular eating place.

Since that experience, my wife always asks, "How many parties are on the waiting list ahead of us?" If the host or hostess doesn't respond with an acceptable number, we go elsewhere.

119

Outsmart Airport Congestion

Dropping someone off at a busy airport or making a pickup? Consider this time-saving alternative to getting stuck in long traffic lines.

A friend in Los Angeles discovered that most morning traffic at major airports consists largely of departing passengers while the opposite is true in the afternoon and evening. That's when more incoming or arriving passengers fill the concourses.

If my friend is dropping off a departing passenger for a morning flight, he follows the arrows and signs to the "Arrivals" ramp and discharges his passenger at the "Arrivals" entrance, usually situated on a lower level. It's no major inconvenience. His passenger takes an elevator or escalator up to the "Departure" level and checks in there. My friend drives off, having avoided the headaches of a congested "Departure" ramp.

In the afternoons and evenings, by prearrangement, he picks up his arriving passengers from the "Departure" level, where the traffic is usually lighter at that time of day.

Simple.

Buying Houses and Investments

120

Beware of the Handyman Special

One of the biggest misconceptions about buying a house is that a fixer-upper saves you money. Nothing could be farther from the truth. Actually, it will cost you more in the long run.

I've been a minor player in rental property for more than twenty-five years and several hard experiences have taught me that a buyer is better off waiting for a "Pride of Ownership" property in a desirable neighborhood to come onto the market than falling into the fixer-upper trap.

"Pride of Ownership" houses account for perhaps one in ten or one in twenty of all resale houses. But they are out there and clearly worth the wait. Your first walk-through tells you that the owners have lovingly cared for the house, performed all needed maintenance, made improvements and upgraded the exterior and landscaping. Ironically, though such houses should bring a premium price, "Pride of Ownership" sellers rarely receive more than the average market price for so-called "comparable" homes in the same neighborhood.

Quite often when you buy a resale house—even though it's *not* a fixer-upper—you'll discover a lot of deferred maintenance that will become your responsibility. Many houses need painting inside and out, new roofs, new carpeting or other floor coverings. All of these items must be added to the cost of the house. However, rarely will the seller reduce the price to cover such expenses. On the other hand, in the case of the "Pride of Ownership" house, you have no such expenses, and yet you pay almost the same price.

How do you calculate the expenses needed to bring a house up to par? First, your real estate agent will likely recommend hiring a professional inspector. These folks usually do a fair job, but to be thorough I suggest hiring your own experts from the trades. These include a heating/air-conditioning technician, a plumbing and electrical expert, a landscaper, a roofing contractor, a licensed pest control operator, a general handyman and sometimes a tree surgeon. Although these experts are among my regular vendors, I always insist on paying each a fee even if they offer to perform the inspection as a courtesy. That's because if they do find a serious deficiency that causes me to exercise my contractual right to cancel the purchase within the inspection period, I want to be able to contact them to inspect other properties without feeling that each time they need to do it without charge.

Bonus Tip 1: For best appreciation, buy one of the smallest houses in the best neighborhood. Buying the largest house in a not-so-good neighborhood is a bad investment.

Bonus Tip 2: Never buy a fixer-upper unless you are handy with tools and can do almost all the repairs yourself. Usually, these houses are bottomless pits that gobble up your money without end.

Bonus Tip 3: If the neighboring houses aren't well-maintained, don't buy the house at any price. You can repair and upgrade a house, but you *can't* fix the entire neighborhood.

121

Financial Security

Short of winning the lottery, I've found only one solid plan that guarantees financial security and is within reach of the average individual. It sometimes requires years of hard work and self-discipline, but under most circumstances it will protect you against most drastic economic changes—inflation, recession, stagnation, depression.

The plan is to buy over a period of several years four single-family rental houses in addition to the house in which you live, *and* have them essentially paid off within twenty years.

Your first rental house should be in a solid, middle-class neighborhood where all of the houses are well-maintained and show pride of ownership. Yours should be one of the few non-owner-occupied homes and should rent for what a postal employee or auto mechanic can pay. Buy the lowest-priced and smallest house in the best neighborhood you can afford. If you're buying it as your principal residence, you'll have an easier time with financing. Lenders become wary if you declare that you are buying the house with the intent of using it as a rental. After you've lived in the house for a respectable period of time and fixed it up to your satisfaction, there's nothing to stop you from moving out and turning it into a rental.

There are numerous books on how to buy and manage rental property. One of my favorites is *Building Wealth One House at a Time* by John W. Schaub (McGraw-Hill). You'll find that as you add to your string of rental properties that you'll have paper losses to report on your income tax return due to negative cash flow and depreciation. You will pay lower income taxes and at the same time see your equity increase.

If you can stay the course for a minimum of twenty years, you should be able to count on receiving one "paycheck" per house per month during your retirement. Each monthly rent payment will provide income comparable to your previous weekly income during your working years.

If double-digit inflation occurs, for example, your rents go up accordingly and your standard of living doesn't suffer. I read recently that 93 percent of all retired people sustain a decline in their standard of living when there is inflation. This underscores why you must be prepared for all eventualities. Otherwise you don't have real security.

More examples: If there's minimum inflation, you don't need major increases in rent. And if there's a depression, you will have little debt—if any—remaining. And that's the key: having your properties *virtually paid off*. That way, in hard times, you can afford to rent your houses at rates lower than other owners who have high mortgage payments.

This approach to financial security has worked for me.

122

Maintenance—A Must

Whether it's your car, your house, or anything else that requires periodic service, keep a step ahead of costly repairs. I know people who have kept their cars alive for fifteen years or more through regular maintenance. I also know individuals who have not replaced their furnaces for more than twenty years as a result of regular filter changes and seasonal maintenance.

In contrast, my friend, Chuck, could qualify as a poster boy for "maintenance avoidance." Except for filling the gasoline tank, Chuck drives his car until it can chug along no more. Then, he pays a tow truck fee plus a huge mechanic's bill. He takes the same do-nothing approach toward his other possessions.

The point is that with regular preventive maintenance, infrastructure and equipment last longer and you will save money on repairs and replacement.

In managing rental property, I inspect each house not less than once a year, taking along a handyman whose knowledge and experience are greater than mine. I first check critical areas such as tub and shower stalls. A few loose tiles can allow water to intrude into the drywall and beyond. Can you guess the difference in cost between replacing or re-grouting a few tiles and repairing extensive water damage? It can amount to thousands of dollars.

Whether it's at home or work, you'll save time and money by periodic maintenance of your property. Remember the adage, "An ounce of prevention is worth a pound of cure." It was true when it was first said and it's still true today.

123

House-Hunting Tips

You won't find this on most lists of house-hunting tips, but I believe it's one of the most important.

Whether you plan to rent or buy, taking this precautionary step is a *must*. If you find a house, condominium, or apartment that you like and are prepared to put down a deposit or make an offer, do this first: Visit the area in the evening and on the weekend.

The need for this became clear to me some years ago when I was shown a nice-looking single family house in a suburban neighborhood. The real estate agent took me through the house in midday when most of the neighbors were away at work. I was ready to submit an offer on the spot, but the agent wisely suggested that I wait until I had had an opportunity to observe the neighborhood on a Friday and Saturday night. Wow! What a difference.

I returned the next evening and drove slowly around the neighborhood with my car windows open. I heard music blaring from stereos and people screaming profanities at each other. I saw cars and trucks parked on front lawns. One house sported a fresh collection of empty beer cans near the front doorstep. Needless to say, I made no effort to buy any property in that neighborhood and was eternally grateful to the agent for his advice.

Another time, I revisited a neighborhood on the weekend and discovered seven vehicles—cars and pickup trucks—parked on the property next door to the house I had under consideration. When I had inspected the property on a weekday, there had been no vehicles parked next door. I later learned that seven students shared the house and the rent there. I have since recommended to all my friends that they revisit a neighborhood *several* times before making a decision on whether to buy or rent.

If you're looking for even more protection, consider buying in a deed-restricted community governed by a homeowners association that requires payment of monthly dues. You can look around and quickly determine whether it's run by a no-nonsense board of directors. Owning a rental property in one of these communities also serves as a screen for filtering out problem applicants. When you inform a prospective tenant that there are strictly-enforced homeowner association rules, those who are offput by such rules will quickly move on.

Doing your homework can save you from making a costly real estate mistake.

People Skills

124

Remember Humility

Judging character is often challenging. I could write a whole book on this subject alone. A shortcut to judging character, I found, is that often where one finds humility one also finds good character.

If I were to list the two dozen most wonderful people I've met, I would say without hesitation that all shared that one attribute. They appeared humble. But, that isn't to say that each didn't feel an inner security. Many held records of impressive achievements or occupied important positions in business or government.

I worked for years alongside a shy reporter before I learned from another colleague that this individual had received a Pulitzer Prize in journalism. When I asked him about it, he shrugged it off, saying, "Oh, yeah, that was a long time ago."

125

When 'No' Can Backfire

You can count on people reacting negatively when you say "no" to their requests. So don't say it; provide an explanation instead. In this context, one of the more memorable characters I've known was an official of a national organization. I often had to contact him as part of my work and had heard through the grapevine that he had a reputation for never saying "no."

Sure enough, the first time I phoned him, after hearing my request, he replied, "George, I'd like to be able to say 'yes,' but..." and then went on to tell me why he couldn't grant my request. For years, my office coworkers and I joked about this official's habit of never saying "no." But, it left an impression on all of us.

126

Playing Santa

We all maintain lists of friends and relatives to whom we send gifts during the holiday season. But we often miss people who truly deserve to be remembered—people on whom we count for services.

I have a list of eight to ten such individuals—the handyman, the postal carrier, the newspaper carrier, the landscape maintenance man, the house cleaner, the helpful bank employee, my advice giver (a retired businessman) and a neighbor who often provides me with free passes to sports events.

It isn't necessary to spend hours shopping for gifts for these special folks. Instead, I send all those on my list a small, but delicious, fruitcake ordered directly from a Trappist monastery in Kentucky. Every year, the monastery mails me a printout of my previous year's gift list to which I can add or delete names. In a matter of minutes, I've taken care of the entire chore, charging the total to my credit card. In some years, I alternate and send a cheese basket instead.

127

Try the Side Door

People often give up in frustration when dealing with a government agency or large corporation. That's because they don't know that in any large entity—public or private—"no" doesn't always mean "no." Bureaucrats are notorious for automatically answering questions by saying "no." I've learned that I can sometimes get a positive response by phoning back and talking to a different person, who often provides me with a totally different answer. Of course, I jot down that person's name and work through that person from that time forward.

Also, if I find myself in contact with someone who is not helpful, rather than confront that person, I simply say, "I understand that you have certain rules to follow and that you have helped me as much as you can, but at this point I believe I'm going to need to talk to a supervisor. Would you be so kind as to connect me? And thanks again for your help." Also, many lower-level employees are embarrassed to admit that they don't have full knowledge about a particular subject or that they lack authority to make any exceptions. Rather than admit to either, they will tell you "no."

Supervisors have more knowledge and experience and often can be more helpful. If the matter is important to you, it's worth pursuing until you feel that no alternative remains. Remember, if it's a large organization, try numerous phone calls at the lowest level. Have your spouse or a friend alternate calling, so that you are not seen as a nuisance. If you fail to get what you need at that level, next try the supervisor. Also, try varying your approach, such as contacting branches or field offices. Another successful tactic, especially if you fail to receive a reply to letters, faxes or e-mail, is to mark "second request" or "third request" on the document. If you receive no answer after three tries, write to a supervisor or next higher-up. In your letter, note that you have tried at the lower level and are enclosing copies of your unanswered correspondence. Be polite, but persistent.

In phone conversations, I've sometimes used the following words: "I'm working my way up the ladder in seeking assistance." This implies that "if you don't help me, I'm prepared to take my case to the next level."

128

Helping Smart

People who help others in need sometimes regret their generosity. One pitfall to avoid is hiring some poor soul despite your intuition that this person has serious problems.

You'll be better off if you provide some cash, a bag of groceries, or perhaps a referral to a job training agency. If you bring this person into your business, you risk losing your customers and even perhaps some current employees.

Recently, a tile setter told me that a year earlier he had lost money in spite of having three trucks on the street because he spent so much time correcting the mistakes of his workers.

Who cost him the biggest loss of customers? A brother-in-law, who had fallen on hard times and whom he was trying to help by giving him a job.

The tile setter now works alone, operates profitably and sends his brother-in-law a monthly check to help him out. The tile setter ends up a nice guy and financially ahead.

129

'Can You Hold, Please?'

How often have you been put on hold and been forgotten?

Here's how you can get your phone call through without chiding the person on the other end of the line after being kept waiting. Wait a reasonable length of time, perhaps a couple minutes. Then, hang up and immediately redial the number, politely informing the person answering that you had been placed on hold, but had been inadvertently disconnected.

This way, you avoid placing that person on the defensive, but at the same time you remind him or her that you'd been forgotten. Most often, this brings a reply such as, "Oh, yes, I'll connect you with Mr. Smith right away."

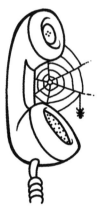

130

Polonius Was Right

There's more truth than poetry in the line by Polonius, the character in Shakespeare's Hamlet: "Neither a borrower nor a lender be." Loaning to or borrowing money from relatives or friends often ruins a relationship.

When someone asks me for a loan, I explain that I have only a limited cash reserve, but that if a small sum would be of assistance, I'd be pleased to help.

In truth, I never expect to see that money again, but I don't tell the borrower that since I don't want to offend. Pay it back when you can, I say, and there's no hurry and, of course, no interest charged.

I probably have been approached for a loan no more than a dozen times in the last twenty years, and I believe I've been repaid perhaps three or four times. I've never worried about any of the "loans" because I never expected a payback.

If the person knows that you recently received a windfall of sorts and comes seeking a larger loan, you can always play "good spouse, bad spouse" (like good cop, bad cop) and say that your spouse won't agree to make the loan. Or perhaps you can say that your spouse already has promised the money to a cousin in Milwaukee or that you've invested it in stocks or mutual funds. People are less offended by such an excuse than to be told point blank that you don't consider them a good risk. It's always an awkward situation, and discretion is advised.

131

Who Did You Talk To?

Have you ever arrived at your destination only to discover that a clerk can't locate your reservation? You say, "But, I spoke to someone yesterday and they said everything was okay." The clerk responds, "*Who* did you speak to?"

I hadn't always made it a habit to write down names of everybody I talked with on the phone, but now I do. I must confess that one of the most satisfying experiences I've had in recent years occurred last fall when my wife and I arrived in Los Angeles and stood in line at a rental car checkout counter. When my turn came, the clerk handed me a computer printout which listed a higher rate than the one I had confirmed via phone. Upon citing the discrepancy, I received the standard, "Who quoted you that rate?" I calmly withdrew from my jacket pocket my itinerary which contained all my travel notes. I replied, hiding my pride, that "On Oct. 2nd at 9:47 a.m., I spoke with a Ms. Vanessa Thomas at your central reservations who gave me this confirmation number 12CHB26195 (fictitious name and number), and not once but *twice* confirmed my rate."

After a brief huddle with a supervisor, the clerk informed me that although this wasn't normally their custom, they would honor the discounted rate I had been quoted.

If you are canceling a reservation and you don't want to find a charge on your credit card statement, be sure to ask for a cancellation number and get a name if possible.

When we're planning a trip, I set up an itinerary on my home computer, which makes it convenient for me to add and delete information until the day of departure. On the morning we leave, I print out three copies of the itinerary, complete with detailed notes—one for me and one for my wife. We also leave an extra copy with our best friends.

132

'Retired'—The Magic Word

Even before I left newspaper work for self-employment, I dreaded filling out applications for credit. Something as simple as requesting service from a utility company or moving into an apartment brought unending questions: "Where are you employed? For how long?"

After I became self-employed, it got even worse. Now the questions were, "You don't have a job? Well, what do you do?" I replied that I was self-employed. I was then asked to submit copies of my tax returns for the previous five years before my application for credit could be considered. And the tax returns had to show that I had sufficient income from my business during that period. Neat trick, if you just left your employment a few months earlier.

My solution to these "Catch 22" barriers? I said "thank you," then hung up the phone and immediately redialed the same number until I got a different representative. When it came to the employment question, I answered "retired." I figured since I had retired from my newspaper job, it was a legitimate answer. Within minutes, the application was completed and I was instantly approved. That was twenty-one years ago. Since then, I have answered "retired" each and every time with identical results. To date, no one has ever asked me from where I'm retired or how long or anything else. "Retired" is truly a magic word.

133

Take It To the Top

When you have a problem with a government agency or large corporation and have exhausted your remedies at lower levels, don't give up. Take your problem to the top.

Although you can get a pothole in your street filled by phoning the city department of public works or get a refund at the supermarket at the customer service counter, when it comes to anything more complex you'll find that middle-management employees are either unauthorized or fearful of making key decisions. They'll often try to cover up for this by saying "no" (as mentioned in an earlier chapter) rather than acknowledge that they lack authority.

What to do? Address your request or complaint directly to the top person. This doesn't mean that your letter will be read by the president or CEO, a senator, or the governor. It probably won't. But, you can be assured that the person responsible for opening the mail in those offices will direct your missive to the appropriate individual, most often with a take-action memo attached. Since the memo comes from higher up, your plea for attention will receive a better reception than it would had you contacted that particular department on your own.

When I have a problem, I try every possible way to resolve it before going upstairs. But when I'm stymied, I dash off a letter to the president. I'm always respectful, rarely critical, and I try to keep the letter brief and to the point. Over the years, I would estimate my success rate at about 50 percent. Not bad, when you consider how many people give up and go away with their needs unsatisfied.

134

Keep a Low Profile

One of the surest ways to turn off a new acquaintance is to flaunt your success. The best-liked and most successful people I know are all careful to maintain low profiles and avoid ostentation. They don't drive flashy cars, wear expensive clothing or jewelry, or boast of their wealth, heritage or social standing.

When I lived in California, I belonged to a hiking club which anyone could join without fee or membership requirement. I became casually acquainted with a number of the regulars, talking, joking and reminiscing with them as we hiked some challenging trails. Often, I would pick up a newspaper and to my surprise see a fellow hiker's photograph on the front page. One was a Nobel Prize winner, another the mayor of a San Francisco suburb and yet another a noted heart surgeon. Each of these individuals could have given lessons in humility. They were unassuming, unpretentious and soft-spoken. Their egos were intact and they didn't need to prove anything to anyone.

Compare that style to the character who gloats over his luxury cabin cruiser, drops names at every opportunity and feels compelled to tell you how much he's worth. The latter is often loud and demands immediate service. Not only does the abrasive guy turn people off, but he also is setting himself up to be charged top price and sometimes more if he is especially obnoxious. Also, these high-profile types are prime prospects for theft, burglary or robbery.

135

Telephone Etiquette

From childhood, it always seemed rude to me when someone answered the telephone and asked, "Who is this?" Often, I've received this response even when phoning a business office. Perhaps, I've been guilty of such rudeness myself.

Then, one day I was seated in the outer office of a city official. With nothing to do but wait for my appointment, I found myself listening to the official's secretary as she answered the phone. In the most polite manner, she would ask, "May I tell him who's calling?"

To this day, even if someone calls at home asking for my wife, I respond, "May I tell her who's calling?" It seems like a more civilized way to screen incoming calls.

136

Hearing 'No' Won't Kill You

Whether in business or personal affairs, taking the initiative is critical. Too often, we fear rejection, so we don't ask. What is so bad about being rejected? Isn't it part of life? Are our egos so fragile that we can't handle a simple "Thanks, but I'm not interested?"

I wish I could tell you how many times I've been surprised, if not shocked, when a business prospect tells me he was just waiting for someone to call with a proposal such as mine. Naturally, there are rejections. But in every deck of cards there are four aces, and you could be dealt such a hand. It's all part of doing business.

In one's personal life it's no less important. As a bachelor, I often found myself hesitant to approach an attractive woman at a social gathering for fear of rejection. Well, I *was* rejected—rather often, in fact. But, I realized that those women were telling me, perhaps, that I just wasn't their type. On the other side of the coin, I realized that I, too, decided when a woman wasn't *my* type. Later, I came to learn that among people in every group, social or otherwise, there exists a percentage of "yes" replies. Though it's a small percentage, it's nevertheless a significant percentage.

Don't allow inhibitions to make you shrink from the challenge. Once you've given this approach a full trial, you'll see that asking for the business (or a date) is not a 100 percent negative experience. Even if your results are only one percent positive, how many of those "yes" answers do you need to make your day? Or your week? Or your life?

137

When They Don't Know The Answer

How often do you go into a store or office, only to find that the person you're asking for assistance is completely in the dark. Yet, he isn't inclined to ask anyone for help. This happens to me at least once a week—either in person or on the telephone. I used to get frustrated, but no more.

Now, a conversation might go like this: "Pardon me, could you tell me whether I need to file two copies or three copies of this form?" Answer: "Well, I think it's two copies."

This person is simply guessing. My immediate response is this: "Thank you. I know you're trying to help me, but, this is very important to me and I need to get it exactly right. If you would be kind enough to put me in contact with someone who would *know for sure*, perhaps I can get the rules on this confirmed. I really do appreciate your help."

People are very reluctant to admit that they don't know the answer. When they're not put on the defensive, they're more willing to help and transfer your inquiry to someone higher up in their organization who is likely to have the answer.

138

Lead 'Em by the Hand

As a newspaper reporter, I was once assigned to cover a municipality administered by a veteran city manager who was long on experience but short on patience. When frustrated by a subordinate's failure to satisfactorily complete a task, he could often be heard to say at open council meetings, in a loud agitated manner, "Mr. _____, I can see I'm going to have to lead you by the hand."

Over the years, I came to understand what he meant. Quite often people don't perform their jobs well. That can be upsetting if you're paying the bills. So, I've learned, when necessary, to "lead 'em by the hand."

If I'm working with people I know and with whom I've worked before, I do not invoke this rule—it's not needed. However, when I order flowers, place a classified ad in a newspaper, or order merchandise by phone, I ask the person taking the order to read everything back to me. I always ask for their names. If I'm seeking information from a government office, I ask, "Now, do I have it right?" and I review the steps. Occasionally, the other party becomes annoyed by my insistence, but I usually manage to fend off anger or criticism by explaining that my wife, my boss, or my customer is prone to worry and I need to be sure that everything is correct. I've learned that when something is important, it makes sense to "lead 'em by the hand." You'll end up with fewer mistakes.

139

Everyone Understands This

Trevor, a family friend, taught me the few special words that can bring extra service or bend a rule when needed. Those words are: "*I would be very grateful.*" For example, if Trevor, who suffers from a bad back, arrives at a destination in a taxicab, he might say to the driver, "I'd be very grateful if you could give me some assistance with this luggage."

It doesn't take a genius to know that there's a tip in the offing. Trevor never flashes cash. He doesn't even mention money or a tip. His technique is discreet, tactful and very effective. It works well in numerous settings.

With his approach, he doesn't risk offending anyone and he doesn't appear crass or insensitive to the pride of others. As a result, he always finds service people very obliging. And he's also very gracious in following up with a "thank-you" in addition to the tip.

140

Appropriate?

If you find yourself fumbling for a word or words in order not to offend someone, perhaps you might wish to add the word "appropriate" to your vocabulary.

I learned this word when I was a graduate student and assigned to a counseling center where the director held staff meetings every Friday. I was impressed with how he managed to correct staff members without offending them. It took me some time to realize that he relied heavily on the use of the adjective "appropriate."

He might say, "John, it isn't *appropriate* to ask these questions." Or, "this wouldn't be an *appropriate* treatment modality." After a while, I found myself counting how often he used the word "appropriate" in a one-hour session. Sometimes it was more than a dozen times. I subsequently incorporated "appropriate" into my own vocabulary and now use it in such instances as, "Thanks, but this product is not *appropriate* for our needs." I need not say more. Seldom does anyone ask me for a detailed explanation as to why it's not appropriate. And it spares me from having to say "I don't like your product or service because...."

There are a couple of other very effective, non-threatening responses that stick in my memory which I use from time to time. If a decision to take some type of action must be made and someone counters my proposal saying, "I don't think we should do that," I calmly and respectfully ask, "How do you think we should proceed?" Or I ask politely, "What do you suggest?"

141

Ask for the Owner

A customer with a complaint should resist the temptation to angrily walk out of a store vowing never to return. In a chain store, sometimes the best you can do is talk to the customer service representative or store manager. But in a small- or medium-sized, locally owned business, there's a good chance you can talk to the owner, who would appreciate hearing from you. After all, if the owner can satisfy you, it may mean repeat business. If you stalk out and never return, the owner will never know about the problem.

When I have a complaint, I'm polite, but always insist on speaking directly with the owner. If I'm told that's not possible and I think I'm getting the runaround from a clerk, I go home and do enough research to come up with the owner's name. I then write to the owner explaining the situation. While many employees couldn't care less whether you take your business elsewhere, the money that you take to another business is coming out of the owner's pocket. He or she *does* care.

142

Wear the White Hat

While covering the courts as a reporter, I once over-heard an attorney tell his client, who was about to appear in front of the judge in a divorce case, that no one—judges included—likes mean or vindictive people.

The attorney stressed that even if someone has the law or the facts on his side, a judge might be inclined to rule against an individual simply because of a bad attitude.

This advice applies outside the courtroom, too. It can affect your relationships at work, in your social life, or even in the checkout line at the super market.

Be the "good guy" and wear the white hat. You'll be glad you did.

143

'Net Takers'

The term "net taker," which I learned when I lived in California, describes individuals who, on balance, take more from others than they give in return. I've known quite a few of them and over time have learned to identify them rather quickly. This is not to suggest that your every action must be a quid pro quo transaction. It isn't necessary and you shouldn't keep score.

Also, a "net taker" shouldn't be confused with a poor soul who's down and out. The latter is seldom in a position to reciprocate. But, the distinction between the two is that the latter is often appreciative and will offer to help do little things or be of assistance in some small way—whatever he or she can do. The net taker seldom offers anything.

144

Getting Even

It's characteristic of human nature to want to exact revenge for the merest slight or insult. But such a reaction is costly in emotional energy and can result in psychosomatic illness. It's usually less costly to walk away from insensitive, uncaring people.

Another consideration is whether retaliation will bring yet another assault by the person at whom you struck back.

People have failed to pay me money owed, failed to deliver services or merchandise, or made very hurtful comments to others about me. In almost all instances, I have decided to write off these people.

Of course, I was disappointed by those experiences and they did hurt. And I suppose I could chalk up some of the incidents to errors in character judgment on my part.

But, I realized I would be better off by simply moving on with my life and not looking back.

A neighbor once confided that she never let any insult or offense pass without exacting some form of revenge or retribution.

"If it takes twenty years, I'll get even somehow," she would often declare. Needless to say, I seldom saw this woman happy.

145

Just the Facts

Unless we are complimenting someone, we would be well advised to keep our characterizations or conclusions to ourselves. Example: You want to return an appliance you purchased for either refund or credit. It doesn't operate properly, it's cheaply made and you have learned that you can do better by purchasing a similar product at another store. Do you say all that to the clerk when you are seeking a refund? Or do you simply show him the appliance, report that it doesn't work and allow the clerk to test it if he wishes?

Does a house painter respond better if you tell him he does shoddy work, or do you simply point out the spots that he has missed? If you must file a complaint with a state or professional board, do you say that the painter is incompetent or dishonest? Or, do you simply detail what happened?

This I learned from my friend, Jacque Fresco, and also from eight years of covering civil courts as a newspaper reporter. The legal system, for example, has no place for conclusions or characterizations. It requires *facts*, first-hand witness *testimony* and *verifiable data*.

Remember, facts are irrefutable. "I did not receive delivery of my newspaper this morning" is a fact. If you contend that the delivery person is "unreliable," you are speculating. He might, in fact, have delivered your paper, but someone might have stolen it. Think before you speak. And never accuse. When you are attempting to get a problem resolved, state only the facts. You can also describe the behavior, but do so in an accurate manner and dispassionately as you possibly can. The less accusatory your tone, the better you will fare.

146

Don't Be the 'Moving Party'

The thought of suing the pants off someone might afford some satisfaction, but that's probably as far as you should go—just thinking about it.

Actually, litigating a civil suit costs money and time, not to mention the anxiety, stress and waiting involved.

The person who initiates a lawsuit is the "moving party" and has the responsibility of pushing the case along. It can take years to bring a lawsuit to trial. All the while you could be paying a lawyer $250 an hour, or more, plus expenses. After all that, the suit might be dismissed or you could lose if it goes to trial. Even if you win, you might never collect a penny if the defendant is broke or has filed bankruptcy.

As a newspaper reporter, I interviewed a man who had a grievance against a government agency. He always carried with him a shabby, tattered box of yellowed papers and files related to his case. He had pursued the matter for seventeen years and had lost decisions at every turn.

But, he wouldn't give up. He returned to our newspaper office frequently and we began to refer to him as "The Man With The Box." It was indeed sad to see that this issue had consumed his life and broken him.

Seek any resolution short of litigation. Often, it's better to walk away and take a financial loss. Ask yourself if the financial loss is as great as what a lawsuit would cost you in time, money, frustration and emotional stress.

147

Making a Change Without Hurt Feelings

For years, I searched for a way to end business relationships with either tradespeople or professionals without leaving hurt feelings. I finally found two effective words that help: "more experienced."

So now, whether it's on the telephone or in person, if I feel I need to end a relationship or if I realize I've hired the wrong person for the job, I have an exit strategy that allows the other person to save face.

I'll say, "I'm sorry. I know that you are very conscientious and want to do a good job, but, I'm afraid that this work calls for someone *more experienced*. I hope you can understand." If any work has been performed, I always insist on paying for the person's time and I thank them. We part on good terms.

148

Support the Family-Owned Business

Whenever I can, I patronize family-owned businesses. By doing so, I not only help keep the American dream alive, but I receive personalized service and often save money, too. And the money I spend circulates back into our community. I do patronize national chains occasionally, but only when it's unavoidable. Have you ever tried telling a clerk employed by a national chain that you've been a loyal customer for fifteen years and feel that you're entitled to some consideration? I thought that would make you laugh! Seriously, though, by patronizing a locally-owned business you establish a relationship that counts for something.

I take my car to a small repair garage where the owner knows me by first name. If I have an emergency repair, he fits me into his schedule. When I phone a family-owned restaurant for reservations, the hostess asks if I'd like our usual table. The same applies to independent lodging facilities, carpet cleaners, hardware stores, locksmiths, etc.

I was amazed a few years ago when a motel operator explained that he can offer rates at about two-thirds what a nearby chain charges because he owns his property free and clear, and he has no debt. By contrast, the chain facility in question had been sold twice in the last several years, so hotel guests were charged high rates to pay for each previous owner's real estate investment gain.

The independent operator often employs family members, so he saves on overhead costs. Also, he doesn't have to pay franchise fees and bear heavy advertising costs, especially if he has longtime repeat guests. In summary, guests staying at a family-owned hotel or resort usually have the feeling that someone cares because the operator is also the owner.

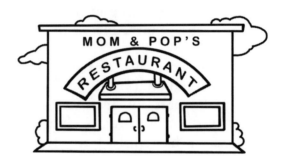

149

Think before You Act!

There's always a price to pay for rudeness, inconsideration, bad behavior or hostile actions. And though this should be obvious to us all, apparently it isn't.

Many folks believe they can tell off their friends, insult their neighbors and say virtually anything they wish to anybody at any time without consequences.

Intelligent people who are preparing to quit their jobs write a letter of resignation in which they give a reason, "to pursue other interests," and thank the company for providing an opportunity for experience.

A less enlightened individual will call the boss an incompetent bum and slam the door on the way out. Satisfaction, perhaps? But, short-lived. And a price to pay? Likely, yes.

In a speech, John F. Kennedy remarked that too few Americans afford themselves "the luxury of thought" before acting. He was right. Think before you act!

150

Take Care of Your Friends

There is nothing worse than feeling isolated, lonely, abandoned, or without friends. For young people, this can be a terrible feeling and result in depression. For older people, it can prove disastrous. How does this occur? Many individuals find themselves either unable or unwilling to make the investment necessary to meet and keep friends. I learned from two persons close to me how important it is to nourish friendships.

All her life, my mother devoted a major portion of her non-working hours to her friendships. She brought together people from her working life, her neighbors, relatives, etc., despite their varying backgrounds and interests. In her retirement years and later, when she suffered from cancer, a day never passed when friends did not either call in person or take her to medical appointments or shopping. For many years after her death, I was in contact with those who told me how much they missed my mother's friendship.

My friend, Bob, who lives in another state, could in my opinion write the book on nourishing friendships. He keeps in frequent contact via phone and e-mail with all his friends and relatives, inquires about their work, activities, health, etc. He makes time to visit most of them regularly and those who live far away at least once a year. Whenever he comes across a newspaper or magazine article or an item on the Internet of interest, he sends the friend a copy with an FYI note. Or if he spots a possible business opportunity for them, he notifies his friends immediately. He is generous, hospitable, caring and loyal. Bob serves as a role model for what friendship is all about.

In contrast, there are those who expect every gesture to be reciprocated. "I went there last week, so it's his turn to go where I want this week." True friendship doesn't operate that way. Rather, it follows the principle of what goes around comes around. Leave scorekeeping for the baseball games.

What's important for me is to know that a friend will be there for me when it really counts. I've been disappointed a few times, especially when I observe someone who has reached the top of the ladder forget his old friends. Overall, I find that next to my wife, my friends are my greatest asset. Without question.

About the Author

George Newman was born in Vienna, Austria. In 1938, his family fled the Nazi occupation and came to the United States. He grew up and attended public schools in Miami, Florida. After serving three years in the U. S. Coast Guard, Newman joined the staff of the *Miami News* as a reporter.

In 1967, he moved to California where he served on the staffs of the *Redwood City Tribune*, *Burlingame Advance-Star* and *San Jose Mercury News*, taking time in between to earn a bachelor's degree. He subsequently received a master of science (psychology) degree from the University of Wisconsin-Milwaukee in 1973. He also served as a part-time faculty member at West Valley College in Saratoga, California from 1973 to 1983.

Among notable achievements, Newman has received the American Political Science Association Award for Distinguished Reporting of Public Affairs; San Francisco Press Club, best news story; South Bay Press Club, best feature story; the Associated Press News Executives Conference, best feature story; and the State Bar of California's Golden Medallion Media Award for outstanding reporting on the administration of justice.

He has been a volunteer in Big Brothers, a Little League coach and rental housing mediator for the City of Mountain View, California. He also served as a trip leader for the Sierra Club and a tutor for Literacy Volunteers of Pima County. He is the founder of Project: One Hour/One Child, a volunteer tutoring program for low-income and at-risk children and is the author of *101 Ways To Be A Long-Distance Super-Dad...or Mom, Too!*

Newman lives in Tucson, Arizona, and he continues to write.